MACRAMÈ

Forty-Nine Beginner's Projects and Patterns to Learn Knotting In A Few Days in An Easy, Inexpensive and Fun Way. Make Your Modern Decor for Your Home, Relax and Switch Off from The World.

NANCY HARRIS

© Copyright 2020 - All rights reserved.

The content contained within this book may not be reproduced, duplicated or transmitted without direct written permission from the author or the publisher.

Under no circumstances will any blame or legal responsibility be held against the publisher, or author, for any damages, reparation, or monetary loss due to the information contained within this book. Either directly or indirectly.

Legal Notice

This book is copyright protected. This book is only for personal use. You cannot amend, distribute, sell, use, quote or paraphrase any part, or the content within this book, without the consent of the author or publisher.

Disclaimer Notice

Please note the information contained within this document is for educational and entertainment purposes only. All effort has been executed to present accurate, up to date, and reliable, complete information. No warranties of any kind are declared or implied. Readers acknowledge that the author is not engaging in the rendering of legal, financial, medical or professional advice. The content within this book has been derived from various sources. Please consult a licensed professional before attempting any techniques outlined in this book.

By reading this document, the reader agrees that under no circumstances is the author responsible for any losses, direct or indirect, which are incurred as a result of the use of information contained within this document, including, but not limited to, — errors, omissions, or inaccuracies.

Table Of Contents

INTRODUCTION 8
    WHAT IS MACRAMÉ? 8
    THE HISTORY OF MACRAMÉ 10
    MACRAMÉ IN THE NEW CENTURY 10

CHAPTER 1: WHAT DO YOU NEED FOR MACRAMÉ? 12
    NATURAL MATERIALS 12
    SYNTHETIC MATERIALS 12
    CORD MEASUREMENT 12
    CORD PREPARATION 13
    FINISHING TECHNIQUES 14
    ADDING CORDS 15
    TIPS FOR CHOOSING AND MEASURING STRINGS OF MACRAMÉ CORD 15
    HANDLING CORD SIZES 16
    PROJECT PROBLEM AS WELL AS SIZING 16

CHAPTER 2: TERMINOLOGIES USED 18
    ALTERNATING 18
    ADJACENT 18
    ALTERNATING SQUARE KNOTS (ASK) 18
    BAR 19
    BAND 19
    BUTTONHOLE (BH) 19
    BUTTON KNOT 19
    BUNDLE 19
    BRAIDED CORD 19
    BRAID 20
    BODY 20
    BIGHT 20
    CROOK 20
    CORE 20
    CORD 21
    COMBINATION KNOT 21
    CLOISONNÉ 21
    CHINESE CROWN KNOT 21
    CHARM 21
    DOUBLED 21
    DOUBLE HALF HITCH (DHH) 22
    DIAMETER 22
    DIAGONAL 22
    EXCESS MATERIAL 22

FUSION KNOTS	22
FRINGE	23
FLAX LINEN	23
FINISHING KNOT	23
FINDINGS	23
GEMSTONE CHIPS	23
HORIZONTAL	23
HOLDING CORD	24
HITCH	24
INVERTED	24
INTERLACE	24
MICRO-MACRAMÉ	24
METALLIC	24
MOUNT	25
NETTING	25
NATURAL	25
ORGANIZE	25
PICOT	25
PENDANT	26
SYNTHETIC	26
SYMMETRY	26
STANDING END	26
TEXTURE	26
TENSION OR TAUT	26
VERTICAL	27
WORKING END	27
WEAVE	27
CHAPTER 3: BASIC AND ADVANCED KNOTS	**28**
SQUARE KNOT AND IT'S VARIATIONS (SQUARE KNOT SINNET)	28
MACRAMÉ MULTISTRAND	40
HALF-HITCH AND IT'S VARIATIONS (VERTICAL, DIAGONAL, BRAID WITH HALF-HITCH)	40
CHAPTER 4: MORE BASIC AND ADVANCED KNOTS	**44**
DOUBLE HALF-HITCH	44
OVERHAND KNOT	47
LARK'S HEAD KNOT AND IT'S VARIATIONS (REVERSE LARK'S HEAD KNOT, LARK'S HEAD KNOT)	47
CHAPTER 5: MACRAMÉ KNOTS	**54**
HALF KNOT	54
JOSEPHINE KNOT/DOUBLE COIN KNOT	54
PROSPERITY KNOT	56
REEF KNOT (OR SQUARE KNOT)	56
CHAPTER 6: HOW TO READ THE PATTERN?	**58**
SIMPLE MACRAMÉ PATTERNS FOR BEGINNERS	58
ORIGINAL MACRAMÉ WEAVING PATTERNS	60

CHAPTER 7: PATTERNS AND PROJECTS I 64
    1   Macramé Bracelet Patterns 64
    2   Jewelry 68
    3   Macramé Tote Bag 69
    4   Knotted Chevron Headband 70
    5   Belt 71
    6   Keychain 72
    7   Hoop Earrings 73

CHAPTER 8: PATTERNS AND PROJECTS II 76
    8   Hemp Yoga Mat 76
    9   Wool Ring Scarf 76
    10   Brooch 76
    11   Dip Dye Macramé DIY Piece 78
    12   Strap of Guitar 79

CHAPTER 9: PATTERNS AND PROJECTS III 82
    13   Butterfly 82
    14   Macramé Necklace 83
Home Accessories 84
    15   Modern Macramé Hanging Planter 84
    16   Plant Hanger Ayla 88
    17   Plant Hanger Bella 94
    18   Plant Hanger Cathy 100

CHAPTER 10: PATTERNS AND PROJECTS IV 108
    19   Simple Modern DIY Macramé Wall Hanging 108
    20   Curtain (For Kitchen, Shower, Etc.+ Variations: Ex: Pendant) 109
    21   Macramé Shower Curtain 111
    22   Table Runner 112

CHAPTER 11: PATTERNS AND PROJECTS V 116
    23   Round Mat (For Table) 116
    24   Hammock 117

CHAPTER 12: PATTERNS AND PROJECTS VI 122
    25.   Lantern 122
    26.   Lamp Wire 122
    27   Sunscreen Macramé Holder 123
    28.   Yarn Garland 123
    29.   Bunting 124
    30.   Mini Macramé Succulent Egg Decorations 125
Christmas Ornaments 126
    31.   Boho Christmas Tree 126
    32.   Tassels 127

CHAPTER 13: PATTERNS AND PROJECTS VII 128

33. FRINGE PILLOW COVER 128
34. TIE BACKS 130
35. HANGING SHELF 131
36. DREAMCATCHER (TREE OF LIFE) 132
37. FELTED IPOD COZY POUCH 133
38. COASTER 133

CHAPTER 14: PATTERNS AND PROJECTS VIII 134

39. DECKCHAIR 134
40. WINDOW VALANCE 134
41. FEATHERS 135
42. MASON JAR 139
43. POM POM HANGING MACRAMÉ 140

CHAPTER 15: PATTERNS AND PROJECTS IX 146

44. DIY CAMERA HOLDER 146
45. "OWL" - A BEAUTIFUL BOARD WITH ITS OWN HANDS MADE OF THREAD 147
46. MACRAMÉ FLOWER VASE HANGER 153
47. SCANDINAVIAN KNOTTED TRIVET 154
48. TOILET PAPER HOLDERS 155

CHAPTER 16: PATTERNS AND PROJECTS X 156

49. INDOOR SWING 156

CHAPTER 17: PATTERNS AND PROJECTS XI 158

50. HEART KEYCHAIN 158

CHAPTER 18: TIPS AND TRICKS 166

USING DECENT QUALITY ROPE 166
KEEP IT SIMPLE 167
KEEP YOUR TENSION EVEN 167
GET INVOLVED AND HAVE FUN 167
ATTEND A WORKSHOP 167
SAVE YOUR LEFT-OVER CORD 168
SAVE YOUR MONEY 168

CHAPTER 19: HOW TO START A MACRAMÉ BUSINESS 170

DO YOUR RESEARCH: 170
KNOW YOUR COMPETITION: 170
KNOW YOUR CUSTOMERS: 170
CREATE YOUR OWN WEBSITE: 170
TAKE GREAT PICTURES: 171
ORGANIZE THE SHIPPING: 171
HOW TO PRICE YOUR ITEMS? 171

CONCLUSION 174

NANCY HARRIS

Introduction

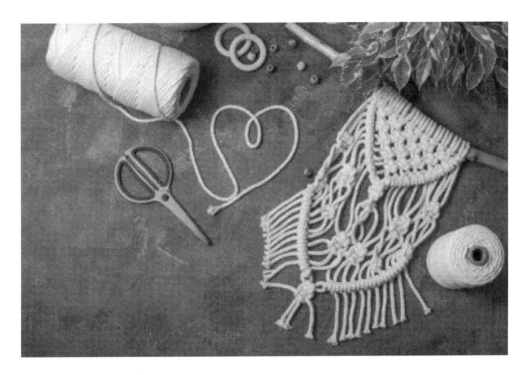

WHAT IS MACRAMÉ?

Macramé is defined as the art of knotting string in a decorative pattern. It is a French word meaning knot and is believed to be one of the oldest forms of art.

Macramé is done by hand, without needles or a machine. The patterns are made by intricately tying and knotting string in a particular manner to achieve the knot you are after. There are over 50 different types of Macramé knots.

The Art of Macramé

For men and women who would like to grasp how-to macramé, there is a range of areas available on the marketplace. Creating complex knots that produce whole patterns that could likewise be transformed into exquisite bracelets, flower baskets, and decorative wall-hangings is just what macramé is based on being an art. The exact first and elaborate step in looking to understand just how exactly to macramé is understanding the basic knots and a couple of diagrams.

Exactly What Macramé Jobs Can I Make?

Decide exactly what job you may wish to create. Look over pictures of Macramé on the Web. It is possible to hunt Esty, Pinterest, along with google. Do some research to master everything exactly is available on the marketplace.

What sorts of Macramé activities will I produce? Start small.

- Plant holder
- Jewelers such as choker necklaces or bracelets
- Wall-hanging
- Novel mark
- Key string
- Bigger jobs comprise:
- Dining table
- Hammock (rescue a significant job such as this)
- Lighting-fixture
- Carpet
- Headboard
- Garland or bunting

Choose the job type. Wall-hangings and plant holders will most likely be both common newcomer tasks.

Where is it planning to be located? This can help determine what dimensions you are attempting to produce.

Locate a design that suits you. Longer free form and organic or symmetric with traces that can be made into fresh and readily defined patterns?

THE HISTORY OF MACRAMÉ

Macramé is believed to have started as early as the 13th century in the Western Hemisphere with Arab weavers. They would knot the excess yarn and threads on the ends of hand-loomed fabrics for towels, veils, and shawls into decorative fringes. What I found interesting is that sailors were the ones to make this popular and were credited with spreading this art form to different countries through the ports they would stop in. They would decorate the handles of knives, bottles, and other items available on the ship and use them to barter for something they wanted or needed when they reached land.

The word "macramé" is Arabic and means "fringe."

Throughout the centuries, the macramé spread across East and Europe, in part due to the practice of tying knots to services and decorations of mariners and merchants.

Macramé methods in the Middle Ages were used to produce gems from human hair that persisted into the 19th century. In England, macramé was a daily and fashionable spare time for lace, decorative details, and clothing dating from the Victorian period.

The interest in knitting art with wall hangings, macramé plant hangers, accessories, and jewelry grew again in the sixties and seventies. Bold patterns and bright colors are a distinctive characteristic of the time.

Jewelry is often made by combining knots with beads, shells, rings, or gemstones. If you take a look at most of the friendship bracelets worn by school children you will notice that they have been made using Macramé.

The enthusiasm for Macramé seemed to fade for a while but was made popular again in the 1970s by the American neo-hippies and grudge crowd in making jewelry.

Macramé is a fun craft to try and you can get started with a small budget. There are a lot of free or reasonable patterns available and some great how-to books to help you get started. This would be a perfect craft to get your children, grandchildren, or anyone involved in.

MACRAMÉ IN THE NEW CENTURY

In the 1970s, macramé was a common textile that was converted into the baton, slings, corner plant, picture frames, wall hangings, hammocks, and even bikinis. Although interest waned after the 1970s, new attention has recently ignited in DIY tutorials for YouTube and blogger's personal websites.

Residents of apartments regard macramé as particularly good because they can increase the quantity of hanging house plants in their room as a solution to the lack of a courtyard.

Today, macramé provides an amazing collection of home and fashion accessories. Macramé affects fashion and house, beginning with hangers to woven tote bags.

Today, macramé has brighter, calmer shades and a wider variety of fibers, texture, and decorations. Macramé is a good solo design – you only need a cord length, two scissors, pins, and a working surface so that it is well moved and stored.

CHAPTER 1:

What Do You Need for Macramé?

Macramé stylists make use of different types of materials. The materials can be classified in two major ways: natural materials and synthetic materials.

NATURAL MATERIALS

The qualities of natural materials differ from synthetic material and knowing these qualities would help you to make better use of them. Natural cord materials existing today include Jute, Hemp, Leather, Cotton, Silk, and Flax. There are also yarns made from natural fibers. Natural material fibers are made from plants and animals.

SYNTHETIC MATERIALS

Like natural materials, synthetic materials are also used in macramé projects. The fibers of synthetic materials are made through chemical processes. The major ones are nylon beading cord, olefin, satin cord, and parachute cord.

CORD MEASUREMENT

Before you can embark on a macramé project, it is essential that you determine the amount of cord you will need. This includes knowing the length of the required cord and the total number of materials you must purchase.

Equipment: to measure, you will need a paper for writing, pencil, tape rule and calculator. You would also need some basic knowledge of unit conversion.

Measuring Width

The first thing to do is to determine the finished width of the widest area of your project. Once you have this width, pencil it down.

Next, determine the actual size of the materials, by measuring its width from edge to edge.

You can then proceed to determine the type of knot pattern you wish to use with the knowledge of the knot pattern. You must know the width and spacing (if required) of each knot. You should also determine if you want to add more cords to widen an area or if you would be needing extra cords for damps.

With the formula given above, calculate and determine the circumference of the ring of your designs.

Determine the mounting technique to be used. The cord can be mounted to a dowel, ring, or other cord. Folded cords affect both the length and width of the cord measurement.

Cord Preparation

Though usually rarely emphasized, preparation of the cords and getting them ready for use in Macramé projects is one of the core pillars of the art of Macramé. At times, specialized processes such as conditioning and stiffening of cords need to be carried out before Macramé projects can be begun. In general, however, cord preparation in Macramé is mainly concerned with dealing with cut ends and preventing these ends from unraveling during the project. During a project, constant handing of materials can distort the ends which can end up having disastrous consequences on your project. Before starting your project, if you do not appropriately prepare special kinds of cords, like ones that were made by the twisting of individual strands, that cord is likely to completely come apart, effectively destroying your project.

Therefore, cord preparation is extremely and incomparably important to the success of any Macramé project, the preparation of each cord is meant to be done during the first step of making any knot, which is the step where you cut out your desired length of cord from the larger piece.

For cord conditioning, experts recommend rubbing beeswax along the length of the cord. To condition your cord, simply get a bit of beeswax, let it warm up a bit in your hands, and rub it along the cord's length. This will help prevent unwanted tight curls on your cord. Note that beeswax may be applied to both natural and synthetic materials. For synthetic materials, however, only Satin and fine Nylon beading cords compulsorily require conditioning. After conditioning, inspect your cords for any imperfections and discard useless pieces to ensure the perfection of your project. After conditioning, then comes the actual process of cord preparation. Cords can be prepared (i.e. the ends can be prevented from fraying) using a flame, a knot, tape, and glue.

To prevent unraveling of your cord using a flame, firstly test a small piece of the material with the flame from a small lighter. The material needs to melt, not burn. If it burns, then such a cord is not suitable for flame preparation. To prepare using a flame, simply hold the cord to the tip of the flame for 2 to 5 seconds, make sure the cord does not ignite but melts. Flame preparation is suitable for cords made from olefin, polyester, and nylon, and the process is compulsory for the preparation of parachute cords. Tying knots at the end of the cord is another effective method to prevent fraying. The overhand knot is an all-time favorite, but knots such as the figure 8 knot which is best suited to flexible cords can be used if you think the knot might have to be undone at some point in your project. The Stevedore knot can be used to prevent fraying when using slippery materials.

Glue is another priceless alternative that can be used to efficiently prevent fraying at the ends of cords. However, not all kinds of glue may be used in cord preparation. Only certain brands, such as the Aleen's Stop Fray may be used in cord preparation. Household glue might also be used, but only when diluted with water. TO prepare your cord, simply rub the glue on the ends of the material and leave it to dry. If you intend to pass beads over the glued end, roll the cord's end between your fingers to make it narrower as it dries. Nail polish may also be used as an alternative to glue. A special class of Macramé cords, known as a parachute cord, requires a special form of preparation. Parachute cords are composed of multiple core yarns surrounded by a braided sleeve. To prepare a parachute cord (also called a Paracord), pull out the core yarns from the sleeve, and expose the yarns by about half an inch. Now cut the core yarns back, so that they become even with the outer sleeve, and then push the sleeve forward till the yarns become invisible. To complete the preparation, apply flame to the outer sleeve till it melts, and then press the handle of your lighter onto the sleeve while it is still warm to flatten the area and keep it closed. The melted area will look darker and more plastic than the rest of the material.

FINISHING TECHNIQUES

Finishing techniques refer to the methods by which the ends of cords after knots have been created may be taken care of to give a neat and tidy project. Finishing is often referred to as tying off. Several finishing knots are available and are extremely effective methods for executing finishing processes. Reliable finishing knots include the overhand knot and the barrel knot.

Folding techniques are also dependable finishing techniques. For flexible materials like cotton, all you need to do is fold the ends flat against the back surface and add glue to the ends to hold them in place. For less flexible materials, fold the cords to the back, then pass them under a loop from one or more knots, and then apply glue, allow it to dry, and cut off excess material.

Finally, you can do your finishing with the aid of fringes. You may choose between a brushed fringe and a beaded fringe.

ADDING CORDS

During Macramé projects, you would constantly be faced with the need to add a cord to an existing cord or any other surface such as a ring or a dowel. The process of adding cords to surfaces is usually called mounting. To add extra cords to a ring or dowel, the most common technique to use is the Reverse Larks Head Knot. When adding cords to already existing cords in use, however, the new cords must blend into the overall design.

To prevent lopsidedness of the pattern, it is also important to add an equal number of cords to both sides in some projects. It is also important to avoid gaps when adding new cords. You can add new cords to an already existing cord using the square knot, the linked overhand knot, and of course the regular overhand knot. Other techniques used for adding cords include the diamond stitch and the triangle knot.

TIPS FOR CHOOSING AND MEASURING STRINGS OF MACRAMÉ CORD

Learn how to purchase the correct type of macramé cable, how to measure the correct amount of cable to use, and how to properly tie cables to produce the correct macramé pattern. A design with too tight or too loose knots or lines that are not aesthetically pleasing will undoubtedly affect how the finished piece looks.

If you have experienced running out of cord to work on or have too much line left over, then you will surely understand how important these tips are. The most important information to remember is that, when buying a macramé cord, you should select the correct thickness, as it is a crucial factor. A thicker thread requires more length; a pattern that has many knots also requires a longer cord.

If you choose to use a cord type that is different from the recommended type in the pattern, then you are risking a result that you may not like. However, if you are experienced enough with macramé cords, you can interchange cord types as long as they have the desired amount, diameter, flexibility, texture, and strength.

If you choose to use a thicker cord that what was specified in the pattern, be well aware that you will need to make fewer knots than what was recommended in the design. A thicker cord and lots of knots can make the piece look bulky, even if you use beautiful accessories like beads and pendants.

HANDLING CORD SIZES

Macramé projects typically include making use of many extended sizes of cords, which, throughout working, can become knotted and twisted in each other. To prevent this, cables can be wrapped or wound around themselves and freely knotted to create a convenient length

PROJECT PROBLEM AS WELL AS SIZING

Everyone will undoubtedly knot with various stress, and the majority of macramé tasks allow for this by being generous with the cord called for. This distinction in knotting can also lead to variations in the dimension of the finished project. Measure your piece as you work as well as, if required, adjust the variety of knots or attempt to connect them tighter or less tight.

Many elements can influence just how challenging a macramé project will be to complete. The size of a finished job can make them harder. However, this is not always real. Some large jobs such as plant holders and also bags are significant, however, be made using only a few or basic knots. The number or kind of knots might cause a design to be much more complex to finish, mainly if there are a lot of layout adjustments or switching between knot types. Another variable to consider problematic is the density of the cords made use of.

NANCY HARRIS

CHAPTER 2:

Terminologies Used

Of course, you could also expect that there are certain terms you would be dealing with while trying Macramé out. By knowing these terms, it would be easier for you to make Macramé projects. You won't have a hard time, and the crafting will be a breeze!

For this, you should keep the following in mind!

ALTERNATING

This is applied to patterns where more than one cord is being tied together. It involves switching and looping, just like the half-hitch.

ADJACENT

These are knots or cords that rest to one another.

ALTERNATING SQUARE KNOTS (ASK)

You'll find this in most Macramé patterns. As the name suggests, it's all about square knots that alternate on a fabric.

Bar

When a distinct area is raised in the pattern, it means that you have created a "bar". This could either be diagonal, horizontal, or vertical.

Band

A design that has been knotted to be flat or wide.

Buttonhole (BH)

This is another name given to the Crown or Lark's head knot. It has been used since the Victorian Era.

Button Knot

This is a knot that is firm and is round.

Bundle

These are cords that have been grouped as one. They could be held together by a knot.

Braided Cord

These are materials with individual fibers that are grouped as one. It is also stronger than most materials because all the fibers work together as one.

BRAID

Sometimes called Plait, this describes 3 or more cords that have been woven under or over each other.

BODY

This talks about the projects.

BIGHT

This is in the thread that has carefully been folded so loops could also make their way out to the knots.

CROOK

This is just the part of the loop that has been curved and is situated near the crossing point.

CORE

This term refers to a group of cords that are running along the center of a knot. They're also called "filling cords".

Cord

This could either be the material, or cord/thread that you are using, or specific cords that have been designed to work together.

Combination Knot

These are two knots that have been designed to work as one.

Cloisonné

A bead with metal filaments that are used for decorative purposes.

Chinese Crown Knot

This is usually used for Asian-inspired jewelry or décor.

Charm

This is a small bead that is meant to dangle and is usually just an inch in size.

Doubled

These are patterns that have been repeated in a single pattern.

Double Half Hitch (DHH)

This is a specific type of knot that's not used in a lot of crafts, except for really decorative, unusual ones. This is made by making sure that two half hitches are resting beside each other.

Diameter

This describes the material's weight, based on millimeters.

Diagonal

This is a row of knots or cord that runs from the upper left side to the opposite.

Excess Material

This describes the part of the thread that's left hanging after you have knotted the fabric. Sometimes, it's hidden using fringes, too.

Fusion Knots

This starts with a knot so you could make a new design.

FRINGE

This is a technique that allows cords to dangle down with individual fibers that unravel themselves along with the pattern.

FLAX LINEN

This is material coming from Linseed Oil that's best used for making jewelry, and even Macramé clothing—it has been used for over 5000 years already.

FINISHING KNOT

This is a kind of knot that allows specific knots to be tied to the cords so they would not unravel.

FINDINGS

These are closures for necklaces or other types of jewelry.

GEMSTONE CHIPS

This is the term given to semi-precious stones that are used to decorate or embellish your Macramé projects. The best ones are usually quartz, jade, or turquoise.

HORIZONTAL

This is a design of the cord that works from left to the right.

HOLDING CORD

This is the cord where the working cords are attached to.

HITCH

This is used to attach cords to cords, dowels, or rings.

INVERTED

This means that you are working on something "upside-down".

INTERLACE

This is a pattern that could be woven or intertwined so different areas could be linked together.

MICRO-MACRAMÉ

This is the term given to Macramé projects that are quite small.

METALLIC

These are materials that resemble silver, brass, or gold.

MOUNT

Mount or Mounting means that you have to attach a cord to a frame, dowel, or ring and is usually done at the start of a project.

NETTING

This is a process of knotting that describes knots formed between open rows of space and is usually used in wall hangings, curtains, and hammocks.

NATURAL

These are materials made from plants or plant-based materials. Examples include hemp, Jude, and flax.

ORGANIZE

This is another term given to cords that have been collected or grouped as one.

PICOT

These are loops that go through the edge of what you have knotted.

Pendant

A décor that you could add to a necklace or choker and could easily fit through the loops.

Synthetic

This means that the material you are using is man-made, and not natural.

Symmetry

This means that the knots are balanced.

Standing End

This is the end of the cord that you have secured so the knot would be properly constructed.

Texture

This describes how the cord feels like in your hand.

Tension or Taut

This is the term given to holding cords that have been secured or pulled straight so that they would be tighter than the other working cords.

VERTICAL

This describes knots that have been knotted upwards, or in a vertical manner.

WORKING END

This is the part of the cord that is used to construct the knot.

WEAVE

This is the process of letting the cords move as you let them pass over several segments in your pattern.

CHAPTER 3:

Basic and Advanced Knots

SQUARE KNOT AND IT'S VARIATIONS (SQUARE KNOT SINNET)

Square knots can be tied in a sinnet (a length of knots tied one after the other) or across many lengths of cords to create solid or netting like patterns. Each knot is made using two steps and needs a minimum of three cords. Two cords are needed for tying the knots and a further cord is needed to knot around. The following tutorial shows you how to tie a basic square knot using four cords and then how to use the knot in various forms.

Beads can be added to the knotting cords as you tie. They can also be threaded onto the central cords and then the knotting cords can be carried around them. For very large holed beads all the cords can be passed through the beads. The square knot can be tied individually or in sinnets. Using two different colored cords will produce a simple pattern through the sinnet. This knot can also be tied in various formations to achieve decorative and more complex looking patterns for jewelry making and other items. This guide contains photographs showing how to tie a basic square knot and then illustrates four further ways in which square knots can be used.

These steps can now be repeated to create as many knots as desired.

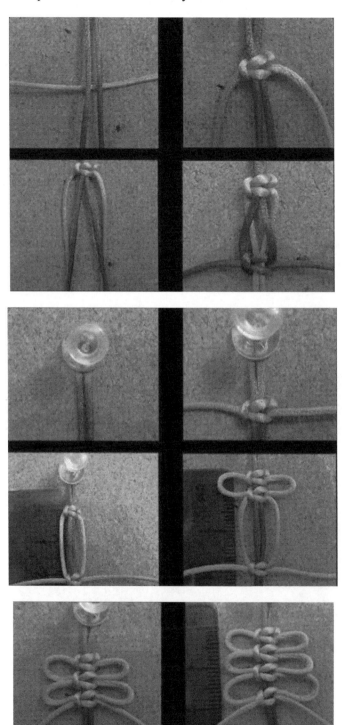

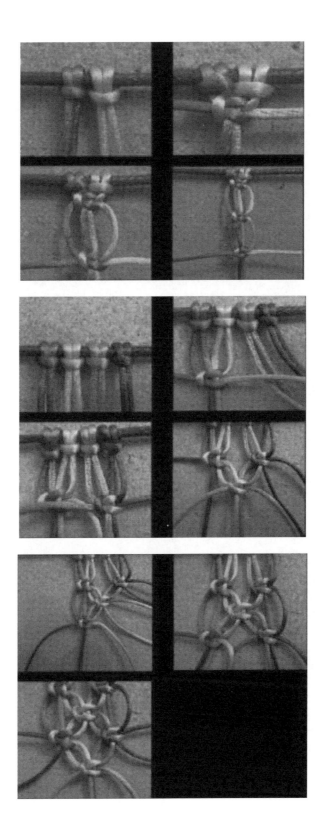

Alternating Square Knots

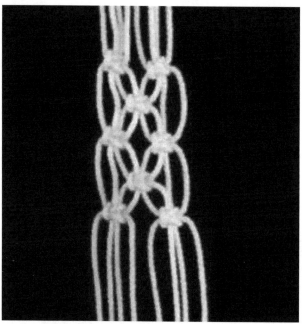

This is the perfect knot to use for basket hangings, decorations, or any projects that will require you to put weight on the project. Use a heavier weight cord for this, which you can find at craft stores or online.

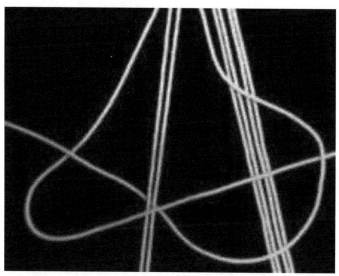

Watch the photos very carefully as you move along with this project, and take your time to make sure you are using the right string at the right point of the project.

Don't rush, and make sure you have even tension throughout. Practice makes perfect, but with the illustrations to help you, you'll find it's not hard at all to create.

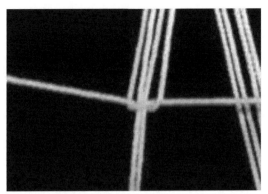

Start at the top of the project and work your way toward the bottom. Keep it even as you work your way throughout the piece. Tie the knots at 4-inch intervals, working your way down the entire thing.

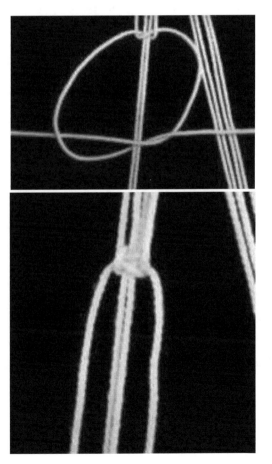

Tie each new knot securely before you move on to the next one. Remember that the more even you get the better it is.

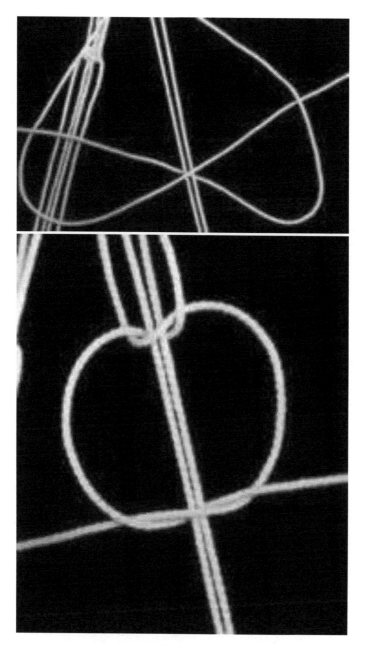

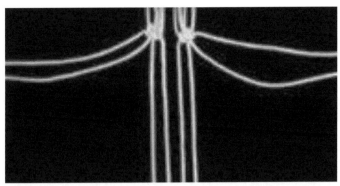

Work on one side of the piece first, then tie the knot on the other side. you will continue to alternate sides, with a knot joining them in the middle, as you can see in the next photo.

Again, keep this even as you work throughout.

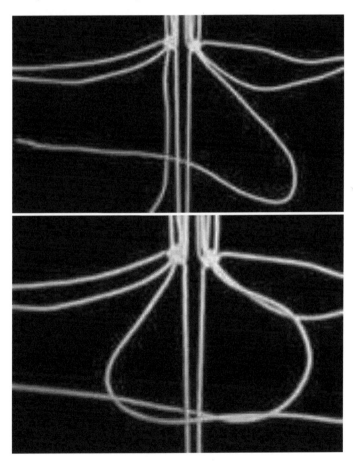

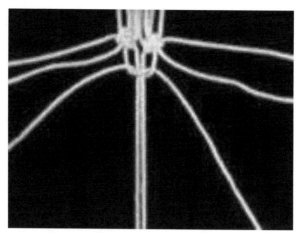

Bring the knot in toward the center and make sure you have even lengths on both sides of the piece.

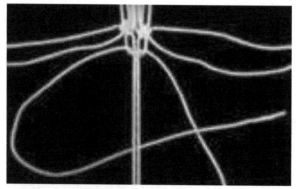

Pull this securely up to the center of the cord, then move on to the next section on the cord.

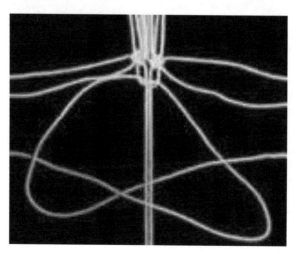

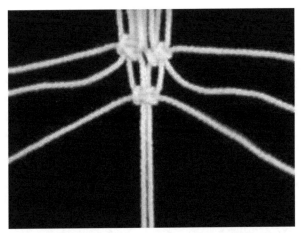

You will gather the cord on one side for the next set of knots, then you will go back to the other side of the piece to work another set of knots on the other side.

Work this evenly, then you will come back to the center.

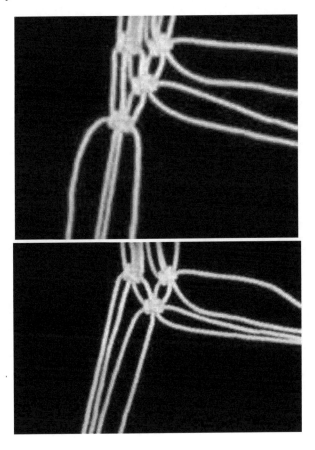

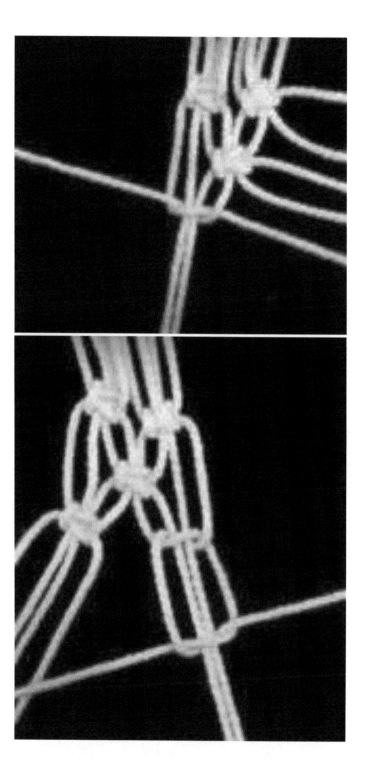

It's a matter of sequence. Work on the one side, then go back to the beginning, then go back to the other side once more. Continue to do this for as long as your cords are, or as long as you need for the project.

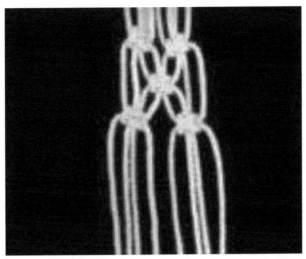

For the finished project, make sure that you have all your knots secure and firm throughout, and do your best to make sure it is all even. It will take practice before you can get it perfectly each time, but remember that practice does make perfect, and with time, you will get it without too much trouble.

Make sure all is even and secure, and tie off. Snip off all the loose ends, and you are ready to go!

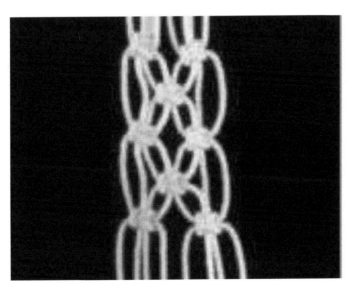

Woven Square Knot

Worked over the four basic threads, this produces a woven effect down the center of the braid. Follow the stage instructions carefully, because each time the cords are not tied as a simple square knot.

1. Knead and twist an overhand knot (see Beginning with a circle, step 2).

    * Take the left cord over the left core cord, under the right core cord, and across the right cord. Pass the right cord under all cords and up through the left loop. Pull ends up the standing firm.

2. Take the right cord below the right core cord, over the left core cord, and under the left cord. Then take the cord on the left under all the cords and up through the right loop.

3. Continue to repeat from * in step 1, until the braid has the required length. Work a regular knot in square to complete.

Square Knot Sennit

This sennit is simply a repeated set of square knots or a continuous sequence of knots. Simple straps or other untwisted knotted chains are often square knot snits.

1. Alternate tying left and right half knots. After the first square knot has been tied, tighten it and start binding the square knots until you have reached the length you want.

2. Continue to the desired length. This is a square sennit knot consisting of 3 complete square knots and one-half knot. Remember that there are 3 loops on the left side of the sennit, and 4 loops on the right. Since those knots were started on the left side, I can count from the left side in following a pattern to keep track of my knot count. Even the loops show you which cord to start next so that you don't lose your position. In this example, I know I must start the next half-knot on the right side by looking at the sennit and seeing 4 loops on the right. This will complete the fourth square knot, which will also have four loops on the left side until finished.

MACRAMÉ MULTISTRAND

You can work macramé with many more cords to create wider fringing bands, a belt, or a cuff bracelet than the basic four. Multistrand macramé can also be used in the round to create products like bags or plant holders. However, you need to plan with more than four cords, work out the design, the number of cords required, and how to secure them to get started.

HALF-HITCH AND IT'S VARIATIONS (VERTICAL, DIAGONAL, BRAID WITH HALF-HITCH)

The half hitch knot is another very common and versatile knot that is used in macramé. Like the square knot, it is fairly easy to learn and can be used to create a variety of designs. Beads and other items can easily be added to either the central or knotting cords to embellish your designs.

Half hitch knots can be tied in two different ways. The knotting cord can be tied either over-under-over the holding cord or alternately it can be tied under-over-under the holding cord. I have included photographs showing both on the following pages. Either of these half hitch knots can be used to tie a variety of formations and I have included step by step photographs for four of these in the following part.

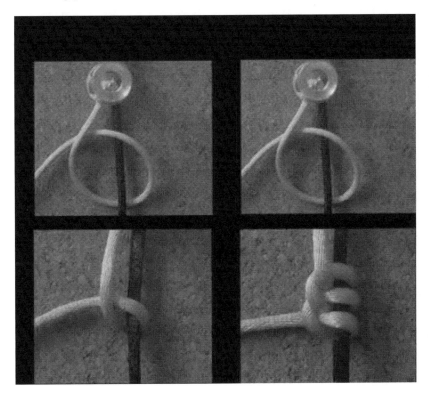

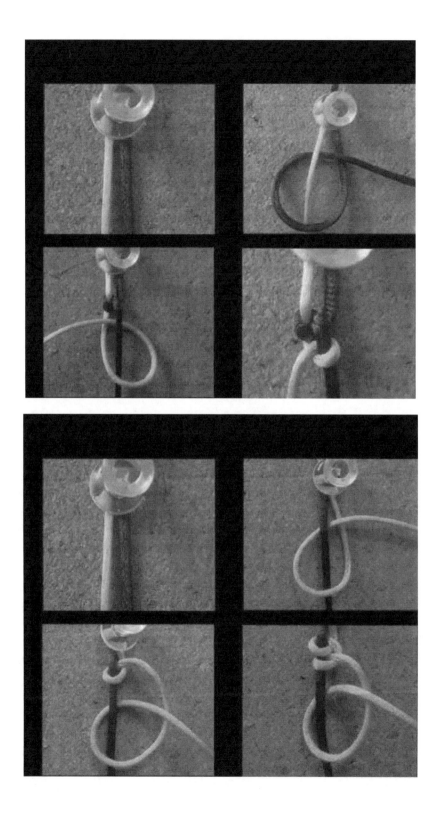

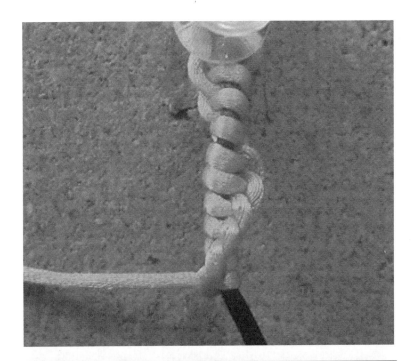
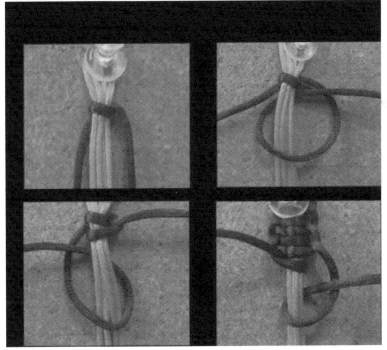

This is a vintage knot that can be used to create wide flat knotted pieces that would be suitable for bracelets, belts, bag straps, and similar. The width of the finished piece is based on the number of central cords used.

CHAPTER 4:

More Basic and Advanced Knots

DOUBLE HALF-HITCH

Double half hitch knots – consisting of at least four cords – are used in repeated sennits to create a perfect visual dividing line as a design feature or, alternatively, as a means of linking separate project segments to form a single unit. The knots are tied around a filler cord, which directs their position, forming elements such as diagonal lines, diamond shapes, or even squiggles.

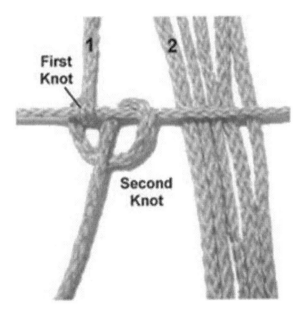

1. Lay knot bearer over working cords

   Mount a mounting cord with at least 4–5 cords with the lark head knots, creating 8–10 working cords. Place a T-pin just below the head-knot of the first lark after cord 1. Lay 1 over all other cords. This is the bearer of the knot or filler cord. The other cords around it would then have each knot. The T-pin assists in directing knots.

2. Begin tying a half hitch knot

   Wrap cord 2 around the filler with a half hitch knot which goes over the filler cord then under and through the created loop.

3. Pull everything taut

   To ensure a well-positioned design element, pull the first knot tight while keeping the filler cord taut.

4. Complete double half hitch by repeating knot

   Repeat with the same cord, another half hitch knot around the filler cord.

5. Tighten double half hitch

   The second knot strengthens and keeps the series firmly in place. Make sure everything is tight and comfortable, and change as needed.

6. Continue across row of cords

   Keep knotting double half hitches from left to right with each cord until you've completed the rows. Note the coil has grown.

Diagonal Half-Hitch

The core cord is pinned straight across when creating a horizontal rib, but if the core cord is pinned at an angle, then a diagonal rib is made.

1. Work a half-hitch rib over the cords. Place a pin at the extremity of the rib. Wrap the side (core) cord around the pin at the angle you want to make, and across the vertical cord. Attach a pin to protect the cord at its root.

2. In turn, tie two half-hitches with each vertical cord to make sure that you hold the rib diagonal while you firm the knots. Ensure that the vertical cords above the diagonal rib are not too loose or tight and that they lie flat.

3. Simply pin the core cord diagonally in the opposite direction to create a zigzag, and operate half-hitches again on all vertical cords. Using the same core cord at the end of the row to head back in the opposite direction once more.

Petal Shapes

The development of all kinds of simple shapes with half-hitch ribs is possible with a little forward planning. A petal shape can be formed by the rib angle and the spacing – using the technique to try out other patterns

1. Secure the right-hand core cord, then take it over the vertical cords and lock, so that the core cord has a slight curve upwards. Function half-hitches along the cord, changing every knot to keep the curve running.

2. In a downward curve, bend the core cord to the left around the pin and around the vertical cords to form the petal. Tie half-hitches over the middle cord to complete the shape of the petal.

Half-hitches are quite sculptural, and the technique applies itself to pieces of jewelry that are very formal.

Endless Falls

This is the name given to the first of the single half-hitch variants as it has the appearance of a waterfall, and the vertical cords tend to spill over and fall behind horizontal crossed cords.

1. Fold one cord around a pin in half, with the U-shaped bend at the tip. Lay the second cord behind you, and work from its midpoint, cross over the ends, first left, then right, so they overlap.

2. Bring the vertical (A) cords up one at a time to tie a half-hitch knot behind the cross-over (B) cords so that the tails finish facing down between the knots.

3. Perform the cord crossing and the half-hitch joining until the braid has the necessary length. Gently pull the cords crossed so that the half-hitches are secure.

Side-By-Side Endless Falls

The two cords (A, B) are bonded together in a slightly different way to create a bold stripe along the length for this variation of endless falls.

1. Make a loop in the middle of a (A) string, so that the right end is on the left side. Place the second (B) cord above the cross point, around the circle.

2. Tie the right end of the loop (A) cord around the loop and then thread the second (B) cord into the newly shaped loop to the right. To tie up the slip knot, remove the first (A) cord and alternately arrange the cord colors.

3. Function as for Endless Dropping, so that the vertical colors on each side of the braid are different. The cords at the crossing will move from side to side.

Chain-Link Endless Falls

The endless falls technique will produce a different texture and pattern by using four or more vertical cords – only work with an even number of cords.

1. Continue the Endless Falls Working steps 1 and 2. Feed a third (C) cord over the two half-hitches and over horizontal (B) cords down from each side of the crossed. Pull the cords crossed to get the knot tight.

2. Then again, cross the horizontal (B) strings, right over left. Function half-hitches for all four vertical cords, pulling down each cord on the half-hitch's right-hand side. Pull the side cords horizontally to keep the knot tight.

3. Repeat step 2, but this time take the vertical cords down each half-hitch on the left-hand side. Continue to repeat these two rows until the braid is the required length, lowering back to two half-hitches at the end.

OVERHAND KNOT

The overhand knot is a very basic single macramé knot. Take a single string to make an overhand knot. Start with a loop over your string. Put the end of the string under the cord and through the loop. Pull it tight, and you're done.

LARK'S HEAD KNOT AND IT'S VARIATIONS (REVERSE LARK'S HEAD KNOT, LARK'S HEAD KNOT)

Learning to make this knot is fundamental because it is the basis for attaching your threads to a wooden bar or other supports. You will only need a ribbon or string. First, fold it in half creating a loop and leaving the two ends of the line together. Next, run the ends through the inside of the circle, and once you're done, pull them together to tighten the knot.

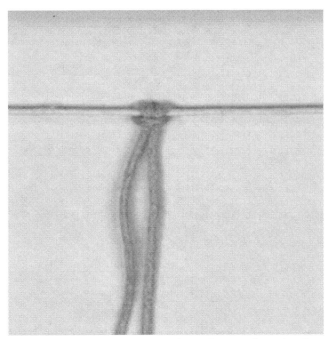

This is a great beginning knot for any project and can be used as the foundation for the base of the project. Use lightweight cord for this – it can be purchased at craft stores or online, wherever you get your macramé supplies.

Watch the photos very carefully as you move along with this project and take your time to make sure you are using the right string in the right point of the project.

Don't rush, and make sure you have even tension throughout. Practice makes perfect, but with the illustrations to help you, you'll find it's not hard at all to create.

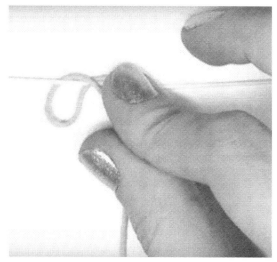

Use the base string as the core part of the knot, working around the end of the string with the cord. Make sure all is even as you loop the string around the base of the cord.

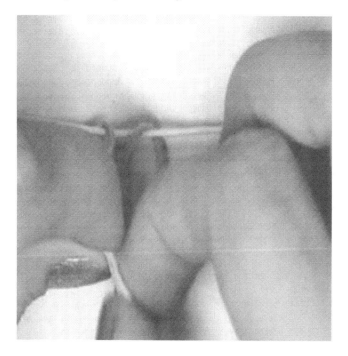

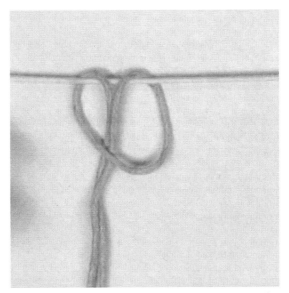

Create a slip knot around the base of the string and keep both ends even as you pull the cord through the center of the piece.

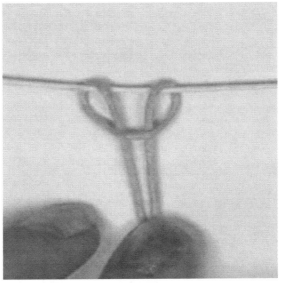

For the finished project, make sure that you have all your knots secure and firm throughout, and do your best to make sure it is all even. It will take practice before you are able to get it perfectly each time, but remember that practice does make perfect, and with time, you will get it without too much trouble.

Make sure all is even and secure and tie off. Snip off all the loose ends, and you are ready to go!

Lark's Head Half Stitches Knot

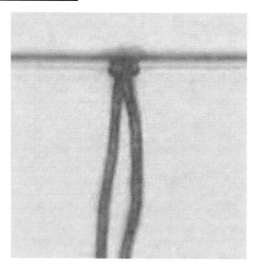

This is a great beginning knot for any project and can be used as the foundation for the base of the project. Use lightweight cord for this – it can be purchased at craft stores or online, wherever you get your macramé supplies.

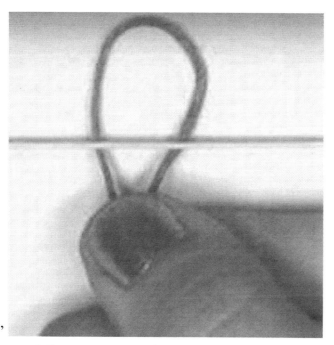

Watch the photos very carefully as you move along with this project, and take your time to make sure you are using the right string at the right point of the project.

Don't rush, and make sure you have even tension throughout. Practice makes perfect, but with the illustrations to help you, you'll find it's not hard at all to create.

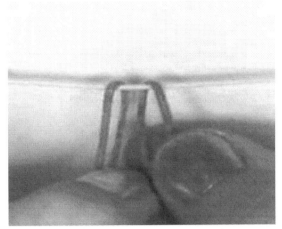

You will work this the same as the lark's head, just going in the opposite direction. Make sure you keep it firm against the base of the cord and work through the steps as you did with the last.

Watch the photos as a guide, following each step as you see them outlined there.

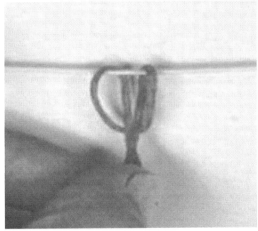

For the finished project, make sure that you have all your knots secure and firm throughout, and do your best to make sure it is all even. It will take practice before you can get it perfectly each time, but remember that practice does make perfect, and with time, you will get it without too much trouble.

Make sure all is even and secure, and tie off. Snip off all the loose ends, and you are ready to go!

CHAPTER 5:

Macramé Knots

HALF KNOT

The double half hitch can knot vertically, horizontally, diagonally, or curved. Usually, this macramé knot is started by placing the materials on the dowel; another method is to tie an overhand knot in each cord, which is then placed onto a knotting board. A horizontal cord is placed across the dangling strands when making the traditional horizontal double half-hitch. Moving left-to-right, the end of the vertical strand is then lifted, and also over the horizontal strand, taking the end from the resulting loop.

The exact end of the same cord is lifted in the same way again. Before getting to the next cord, every cord is knotted twice. This knot can be used on hemp, silver, or other foldable jewelry ties, much like the square knot. The knot of the double half hitch can be strung together to make large chokers, bracelets, and necklaces.

JOSEPHINE KNOT/DOUBLE COIN KNOT

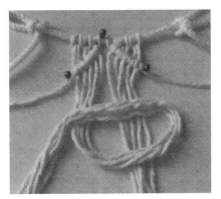

This is the perfect knot to use for basket hangings, decorations, or any projects that will require you to put weight on the project. Use a heavier weight cord for this, which you can find at craft stores or online.

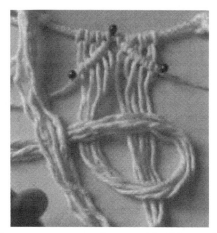

Watch the photos very carefully as you move along with this project and take your time to make sure you are using the right string in the right point of the project.

Don't rush, and make sure you have even tension throughout. Practice makes perfect, but with the illustrations to help you, you'll find it's not hard at all to create.

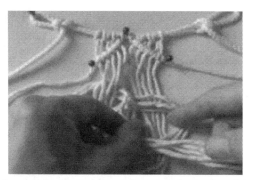

Use the pins along with the knots that you are tying, and work with larger areas all at the same time. This will help you keep the project in place as you continue to work throughout the piece.

Pull the ends of the knots through the loops and form the ring in the center of the strings.

For the finished project, make sure that you have all your knots secure and firm throughout, and do your best to make sure it is all even. It will take practice before you are able to get it perfectly each time, but remember that practice does make perfect, and with time, you will get it without too much trouble.

Make sure all is even and secure and tie off. Snip off all the loose ends, and you are ready to go!

PROSPERITY KNOT

The knot of prosperity is a broad flat knot in the form of a rectangle, which makes it ideal for belting. You can tie only two knots one by one, but inserting a double coin knot in between holds the belt flatter, allowing you to change it with the buckle to a more precise length. You might attach beads between the knots to embellish or hang charms from one or two loops.

REEF KNOT (OR SQUARE KNOT)

While working a reef knot (RK) Cord too wide for tying complicated knots can be turned into a simple and easy pattern, suitable for creating a beautiful bracelet.

1. Cut two 6 mm cord 25 cm (10 inches) lengths and make a reef knot. Correct the knot until both sides are at the same length, then softly tug to firm up our knot.

2. Test the size of your bracelet for buckling, cut the edges of the string, and attach all strings with a good jewelry adhesive at either end of the clasp.

NANCY HARRIS

CHAPTER 6:

How to Read The Pattern?

SIMPLE MACRAMÉ PATTERNS FOR BEGINNERS

Let's start with the basics. To work:

- Material
- Scissors
- A solid foundation

In principle, you can take any thread and even a rope, but the most textures and the most beautiful things are made from cotton.

A solid rectangular object is taken as a solid base: a wooden cutting board, thick plywood, or even a large book.

As you can see, nothing unusual is needed for a macramé; you will create beautiful things with your own hands from what is available. It remains to talk about basic patterns that are easy to perform even for beginners. Here are the stages of preparatory work:

- First, tie a thread over a book or other similar item, the knot should be at the back.
- Now you need to cut several threads. The amount depends on the particular business.
- Cut in half, and they are tied with a threaded strip.

If you want to do a small thing, for example, make a bracelet using a macramé technique, then you can either attach it not to a cross rope, but a safety needle, attached to a needle pad or other similar fabric. Some connect the needles even to their jeans (up to the knee area) and weave a bracelet. But at the same time, safety precautions must be observed.

Let's start with simple patterns that require several threads. They will help fill in the macramé elements of the weaving pattern. You can make a bracelet in this technique.

See how the right and left loop nodes are formed.

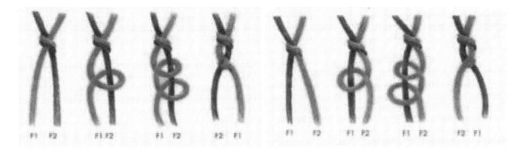

1. Let's start right. F1 is a working thread, and F2 is a thread. We thread the working yarn on a ductile thread, make a counter-clockwise turn, skip the end of the thread into the resulting loop, tighten.

2. Now, in the same way, tie the second node, lifting it to the first, and then inserting the thread to the right below the node. Position the working thread F1 on the right side of entangled F2 and draw the element in the mirror image so that you get a knot in the left loop.

If you want to learn how to make bracelets using the macramé technique, then another one called "tatting" is also helpful with this pattern.

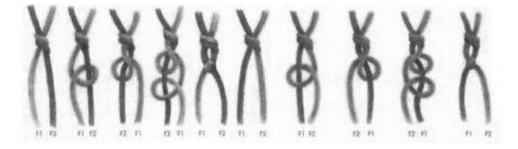

1. Fit working thread F1 on the left and locked F2 on the right. Sew one looped right knot, and then one left. So, by alternating these elements, we weave the chain.

2. The real "punching" starts with the node of the right loop. If you want to make a left tattoo, then start with the left one.

Here is another pattern you can also adopt when making macramé bracelets. It is also widely used for weaving other beautiful things and is called a "square" knot.

You will need two threads for this. Usually, their length is 1 meter. Bend each in half, tie to a transverse thread, or attach to a soft surface with a needle.

In the weaving process, the working yarn is shortened more than the main thread. In order not to build, it is possible to tie the ribbon at the initial attachment so that the worker is larger than the main one.

In this case, the workers are the ones on the right and left, and the two main ones are in the middle. Move the left work thread through the two main ones, but the right thread on it put it behind the main ones, put it in a loop that forms on the left (this node is called the "left side plane").

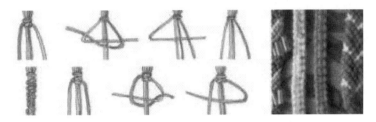

Now repeat the manipulation on the mirror image, starting with the right working thread (this node is called "right-hand flat"). So, by changing the threads, complete the entire chain. It will turn out that the relief was bilateral. If you want to make a twisted chain (such are used for cache, for example), then create only left or right patterns only.

If you change "square" nodes in a checkerboard pattern, you will get a "checkerboard" pattern.

ORIGINAL MACRAMÉ WEAVING PATTERNS

We continue to study fascinating macramé, presenting two more patterns for beginners. The first is a square-knot rhombus. To execute it, you will need:

- Six threads
- A needle or a single thread to secure the work
- Scissors
- Substrate or book as a basis

Fold each of the six threads in half, fasten. You will get a total of 12. See the diagram. For convenience, all topics are numbered.

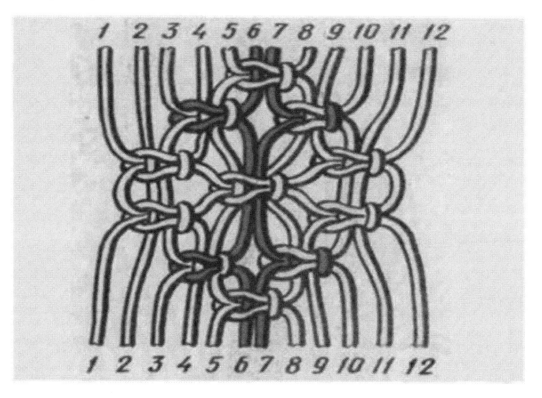

1. First row. From the center - 5, 6, 7, and 8 threads weave a "square" knot.

2. The second row - we create two "square" nodes: the first - of 3, 4, 5, 6 threads; and others - from 7, 8, 9, 10.

3. Third row: two "square" nodes must be woven from 1, 2, 3, 4 threads and 9, 10, 11, 12.

4. The fourth row is similar to the first.

5. Fifth - to third.

6. The sixth line is repeated by the second.

7. And the seventh is the third or the first.

Here's how to create other patterns using the macramé technique. For beginners, weaving patterns should not look complicated, and the following is presented.

Fasten based on four threads, bending in half to get eight.

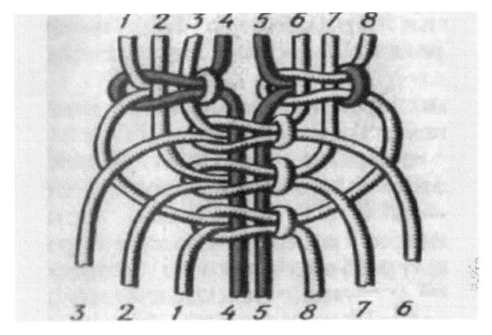

We count the rows to know which threads the square nodes are made of:

1. 1, 2, 3, 4, 5, 6, 7, 8.

2. 3, 4, 5, 6.

3. In this third row, the quadrant pattern will be the main threads 4 and 5, and the workers 2 and 7.

4. One square knot. For him, the working thread is 1 and 8, and the main thread is 4 and 5.

Now you know how macramé is created, about the primary nodes, the patterns for beginners that they use in their work.

NANCY HARRIS

CHAPTER 7:

Patterns And Projects I

1 MACRAMÉ BRACELET PATTERNS

If initially only strands were used in making macramé jewelry, now craftsmen add absolutely all accessories to their work based on their imagination: ribbons, beads, beads, cabochons, buckles, and more.

Also, jewelry using the macramé technique can find such defining words as micro-macramé. The difference between a micro-macro and a macro is that only the finest threads are used for the micro-macramé, and the workflow becomes more tedious, and the difference is visible to the naked eye.

One of the first macramé embellishments is the bright and colorful friendship bracelets, many known as mouline threads.

Now we will show modern macramé ideas that can be found in any type of jewelry: earrings, necklaces, pendants, bracelets.

A master class of bracelets made of string and beads using the macramé technique.

Accessories:

- Nylon or wax cable
- Beads green, orange, blue, yellow

Instruments:

- Scissors

Installation:

Prepare seven pieces of ribbon, 100 cm in length, assemble and bind at the top into a knot. The outer cable is slightly offset, it will be the lead cable, which we will tie the rest.

We take the next rope and first draw it on top of the lead cable, turn it over, tuck it under the lead cable, and put it in the loop. Now we bring it back to the lead cable, draw it on top, rotate it, pull it under the lead cable, and put it in the formed loop.

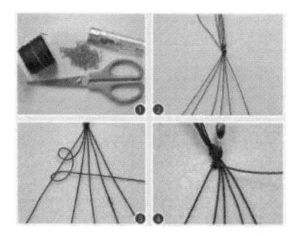

Now we tie the lead cable in the same way, with each other (Fig. 5).

After that, we place the lead cable on top of all the wires in the row and start the binding again, but from below (Fig. 6-7)

Turn the lead cable again and attach the wires to it (Fig. 8)

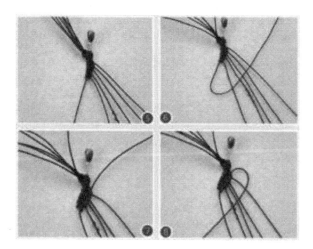

Once again, we connect the lead cable to all cables (Fig. 9)

Now we inscribe each cable except the leading beads in the order as in photo no. 10th

Then we place the lead tape on the ribbons after the beads and the ribbons are made three times (Fig. 11, 12 and 13)

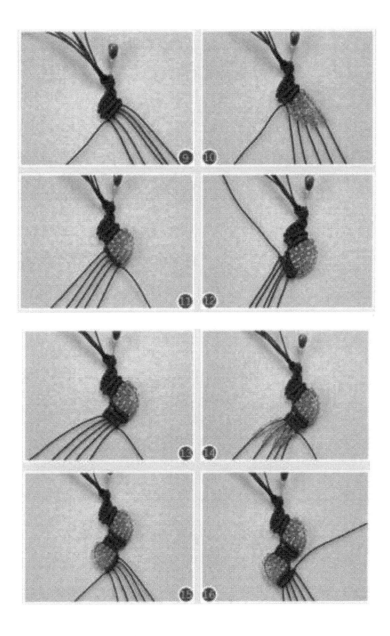

When the desired length is woven, straighten the ends of the cables with scissors and lay them parallel to each other (Fig. 20)

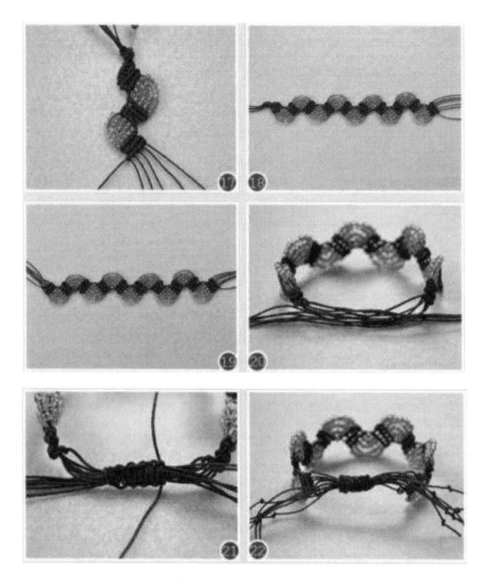

We decorate the bracelet lock in the form of Shambhala knots.

At the same time, we tie each edge of the lace into a knot.

The bracelet is ready!

2 JEWELRY

Armbands Rhinestone

Micro macramé with such a delicate knotting string is suitable for fragile jewelry. Seed bead may be attached to the outer threads to create a basic jeweled strap or attach a very little bling by fastening the strings across the cup string.

You're going need some

- 11-centimeter (41/4in) rhinestone cord (extended)
- m (2/4 yd.) nylon knitted fabric string 1 millimeter

Place the cup chain length on top of the two cord strings. Perform a square knot among each cup chain. Check for the bar just above prior square knot: if this was on the right, the very next square knot with right string would start; unless the bar has been on the left, continue only with left string. Carry on working a square knot across each rhinestone, rotating between sides where you proceed to align the square knots

- E-6000 Jewelry glue.
- Pin pad and map pins (facultative)

Cutting a total of 50 centimeters (20 inches) off the knotting string and slice the two sections in half. Pin or tag with the chain at the edge of the short length to the working board. Connect the good piece of string with an overhand knot from the around the small side.

Perform 3 centimeters (1V8 in) square knots for a 17.5 centimeters (7 inches) length wristband. Place a pin or tag to secure it in the base of the nodes. Complete the macramé with square knots 3 centimeters (1V8 in) segment or operate the span to suit its other side. Test the band size and change if required. Function a 2-strand knot over two cords and loop the strings in combinations. Secure the knot, draw via the loops, and so that it becomes approx. 3-5 millimeters from the square knots. Secure the knot. Place a little adhesive into the knot of the button in which the strings come up at the bottom and cut the strings after the adhesive has started to dry up. Test that perhaps the loop fits snugly around the knot on the other side of the band. You should move the macramé knots down or up the middle of the core cords slightly. Add a little adhesive on the back to protect the circuit in the right position.

Switch the overhand knot to the opposite side once you have connected it to the macramé

3 Macramé Tote Bag

Instructions

1. Cut 10 ropes 2.3 meters wide. Fold half and fill the middle of the folded handle with the void. Take the ends of the rope and cross the last step of the loop you made. Pull close. Pull strong.

    Continue to attach 5 pieces of cord to each bag handle.

2. Separate two rope bits at one end and move the remaining rope to the other. We'll make the first knot with these two parts.

    Turn the left corner in the right corner and make a curve.

    Take the left (still straight) rope and fill the room with the two ropes you made. Remove the two corners until the knot is rising and in the right place. You want the handle to be approximately 5 cm.

    Take the left-hand rope and this time put it right to complete the knot.

    This time, thread through the gap the right-side rope. Bring the knot tight again.

3. Create four more knots in a row on the handle with the rest of the ropes. Then continue again, but the first rope is missing this time and the second and third ones tie. Continue along the route. You make four knots this time and you don't knot the first or the last rope.

4. When the second row is done, make the third row the same as the first (five knots without missing ropes).

5. Upon completing the third section, repeat steps 2-4 in the second handle. After that, bring the two handles face to face together.

6. Take both end ropes from the front of the bag and back to begin the next row. Fasten the ties on the front and back on the other end. You are then faced with the last lines on the front and back. Tie these together.

7. Knead until the strands are approximately 10 cm left of the rope.

8. Cut the length of the rope 4 meters. Use the same technique to tie it to the last knot of the handle.

9. Take the front and back strand and wrap the cord around. Place a double hitch knot and take two additional knots, one on the front and the other on the back.32

10. Taking off the hanging rope. Link these strands instead of knots. You should apply some glue to cover them. Put it together to make a sheet.

4 KNOTTED CHEVRON HEADBAND

Supplies:

- Broder floss (6 colors/12 suits my 1/2-inch wide headband)
- The satin narrow belt – 1/8 to 1/4 "is perfect.
- E6000 or equivalent adhesive plastic
- 1/2-centimeter-long or your favorite headband
- Matched thread and needle sewing
- preferably if you want to place the knotted portion on the headband for extra stability

Instructions

- Start by making your extra-long friendship bracelet.

- I've been using 6 strands each 10 feet in length, half by 5 feet, but if your headband is wider, maybe your headband would be bigger.

- Hold a removable knot together and tie the strands and operate the Classic Chevron Friendship Bracelet (or pattern for you) until the strip is 1 to 5 inches longer than the length of the headband.

- Untie the knot upon completion.

- Put a dot of glue on the back of your headband and put it around your headband. Make sure you cover the band on the front and back and if you have a single face on the satin belt, the good side is off.

- Cut off the tails one end of the knitted strip and hold it down. Save it for a few minutes.

- Put some glue on your back and tie the knotted strip to the rope until it is imperfect.

- So, go on gluing and binding, but then behind the knotted thread.

- Avoid gluing and wrapping when the knotted strip is as far away from the other end.

- Cut the tails to the end and add the whole length of the super long bracelet to the end. Likely, you will extend it a little to match and that's perfect. (Keep it to the end only if you want to stitch the kneaded portion on the back).

- Hold on the end of the strip and tie it smoothly on your back to the end of the headband.

- When you just hang up, you can thread the knotted piece back and forth on the edges and draw it close. This is a good choice because the line has very straight edges.

5 Belt

This project is proof that necessity is the mother of invention. One of our friends was putting together an outfit and decided she needed a black belt, but it needed to be the kind that sits on the hips, which we didn't have. Using a large metal ring and the most wonderful black leather lace, we made her a belt. When we discovered the metal ring was the perfect size but not the most attractive belt buckle, wrapping the ring with leather lace seemed to be the answer. If you find yourself in the same situation, this belt can be whipped up in a flash to suit any outfit—just choose any colors and types of materials you'd like.

6 KEYCHAIN

What you Need

- Wood Darice Tags
- Darice Macramé Cord
- Vinyl
- Darice keychains
- Rit Dye

Instructions

- Cut and dye 6 pieces of cords
- Now you have to add a monogram to the wood tag. Do this using the vinyl letter or paint.
- Trim the top of the wood tag.
- Now put the tag on the key chain
- Now using the lark's head knot, knot the first piece of the macramé thread.

- Repeat the same knot for the second piece of thread.
- Make a spiral knot and pull it uptight.
- Continue making spiral knots until you get your desired length.
- Fray the ends of the work with a comb.
- Cut the tassel straight after the cords below the knot have been frayed.
- And that's a nice macramé keychain

7 Hoop Earrings

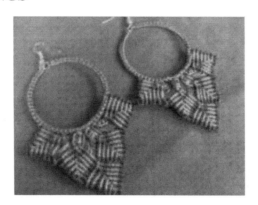

What you Need

- Yarn
- Darice Macramé Cord
- Scissors
- Little hoop earrings
- Clips

Instructions

Step 1. Take 4 strands of thread.

Step 2. Loop the threads over the hoop earrings.

Step 3.   Now make a square knot with the four threads.

Step 4.   Make another square knot

Step 5.   Make one more square knot in the middle to connect the leaders finally.

Step 6.   Comb the ends of the threads to fray it a little.

CHAPTER 8:

Patterns and Projects II

8 HEMP YOGA MAT

We can't help being one of those people that would rather make something we need than buy it. A holder for our yoga mat is just one of those things. Sturdy hemp makes a good strong frame. You could also use a colored leather lace, that adds a pop of color (though you could opt for an entirely hemp project, or use another sturdy cord, like vegan-friendly ultra-suede, in lieu of the leather). This project is created by "macramé in the round," working continuously by rotating the piece and knotting the sides together on every other row. Try adapting this approach for bags of all sizes, from tiny amulet holders to big laundry sacks.

9 WOOL RING SCARF

We have already mentioned our jealously of knitters and all the beautiful yarns they get to work with. We have to indulge in all of the hand-dyed, gorgeous wools and cottons and all of the other yummy yarns available. If we can't knit them, we'll knot them! We chose some amazing handspun variegated wool yarn for this scarf. You need a lot of material to create such a big project, but trust me, the results are worth the indulgence.

10 BROOCH

Macramé is often thought of as a very simple chunky knotting tool, but it turns into an elegant micro macramé when used in fine cords. To create a rainbow effect through this beautiful brooch, select matching colors.

You will need

- 1.5 m (1 3/4 yd) of each SuperlonTM cord in violet, lilac, coral, light gray and dusky pink
- 20 cm (8 in) of 1 mm (19swg) half-hard sterling silver wire

- Seed beads: size 6 (3.5 mm) matt silver, size 10 (2 mm) colored peach, size 11 (2.2 mm) silver-lined crystal and smart raspberry gold luster
- UltrasuedeTM 10 cm (4 in) square
- Brooch back
- Jewelry tools

Instructions

1. Set the SuperlonTM cords ready for use: red, lilac, coral, light blue, and dusky pink.

2. Take on a purple cord a silver-lined crystal seed bead and drop to the middle. Fold the cord in half, and put it on one side of the 'V' over the cable. Take the tails over the wire and through the loop back to form the head knot of a reverse lark.

3. Work on either side of a half-hitch. With the other colored cords repeat measures 2 and 3, adding a bead each time.

4. Lay the outline of the wire on the baseboard of the foam, and place the tape in position.

5. Bring the lilac end cord in parallel to the cable. Act with each cord in effect a double half-hitch

6. Place a map pin at the end of the rope, then take the purple cord back in a slight angle around the vertical cord. Secure with tape or clip on a spring. Work with the dusky pink cords and the first grey cord in double half-hitches. On the next grey thread, pick up a color-lined peach seed bead and again work double half-hitches.

7. Work double half-hitches with first coral cord, then pick up on the next coral cord two silver-lined crystal seed beads; secure with double half-hitches. On the first lilac thread, add three emerald raspberry gold luster seed beads, securing again with double half-hitches.

8. Work double half-hitches on the next lilac cord before finishing with silver crystal, 6 matt silver, and silver crystal on the remaining lilac cord. Run the last half-hitch of the pair.

9. Repeat from step 4 six or seven times, depending on the stress, before the half-circle of macramé curves around to touch again the thread. Again, take the purple cord back to

the outer edge and work straight half-hitch rope. Function double half-hitches over the wire for every cord in place.

10. Tuck all of the silver wire cord tails behind it. Take on the first dusky pink cord two silver-lined crystals, a size 6 matt silver seed bead, and two silver-lined crystals. Function on the other side of the wire 'V' shape a double half-hitch. The next dusky pink cord is attached without beads.

11. Repeat on the two grey cords and then work the wire down, inserting beads on the first of each color, reducing the number of silver-lined beads as the distance between the wires narrows.

12. Work a semicircle in macramé to suit the first line, finishing with a half-hitch rib straight. Function the first cord with a double half-hitch, and add a silver-lined crystal. To secure the bead, work another double half-hitch with the same thread. Repeat with each cord in seconds.

13. Fold the cord over the back of the macramé, and thread with tiny stitches invisibly. Trim sparingly. Cut UltrasuedeTM into place invisibly around the edge to match every semicircle and stitch.

14. Knit a brooch on the reverse side of the brooch, stitching straight through to the right side, then going back to the reverse side so that the small stitch between the macramé knots is covered. Sew the ends tightly into.

11   DIP DYE MACRAMÉ DIY PIECE

To include some color to my piece, I chose to dip color the bottom. Next, put in the liquid color (I utilized about half of the bottle) and mix carefully.

As soon as your macramé DIY piece has actually dried, it is all prepared to hang.

Next, get your macramé damp prior to positioning it in the color bath. I began by positioning simply the bottom 3rd or two of the wall hanging into the color bath for about 10 minutes, and after that, I moved a bit more down for another five or two minutes, then I simply rapidly dipped the last number of inches in briefly to get the lightest color at the top. Wash the colored piece under running cool water up until it runs clear.

For the 2nd row, you will make your square knots utilizing two hairs, each from 2 surrounding square knots (see the image listed below). Now, the hairs that were center hairs in the previous row will be outdoors hairs for this row.

I enjoy the texture you can get with even simply one easy macramé knot, and the ombre color this piece has!

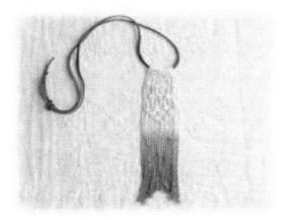

12   STRAP OF GUITAR

One such Macramé design is perfect for an instrument strap to play music for someone who is in your heart. While the instructions may appear a little difficult, the sequence is easy to understand

Materials

- Polypropylene string 100 meters 3.5 millimeters
- Slice 2 samples of 20 meters apiece
- Split out two samples of 19 meters apiece
- Slice two eighteen-meter parts of the string together

Instructions

1. Grab the twenty-meter strings and flip them halfway and pinch the middle to the surface of Macramé. Cut the latter twenty-meter cord in the quarter and connect the Square Knot Sinnet approximately halfway through the first string from the fold on the 1st cord.

2. Connect the 1 V inches Square Knot Sinnet.

3. Lower 1 inch down and bind a further Square Knot Sinnet and continue with 3 V inches of knots. That region of the design is the guitar strip's collar.

4. Put the two strings of 19 yards. Flip each string in half and place one on each section of the functioning strings on the Macramé frame.

5. Count the chord from One to Eight, going from right to left. For knotting strings, use cables 1 - 4, 5- 8. Connect a Knot Square amongst each string band.

6. Bind a Square Knot as the knotting strings for the 3 - 6 strings.

7. Repeat step five and step six five times, ensuring that you wrap up on a one-piece knot.

8. Attach 18 strings in the yard. And by step 4 repeat, Place every string in quarter and place along either side of the active strings on the Macramé panel.

9. Label the string from one to twelve and move from left to right. We should use knotting strings one and four, five and eight, nine, and twelve. Connect a Knot Square with each string band.

10. 10. Knot square to three, six, seven, and ten cords like knotting strings.

11. Repeat the procedure nine and ten to the middle of the guitar belt for one inch.

12. If you meet the very last combination of two square knots, apply another square knot immediately below, and in the middle of the two last knots, you will make a "V" using Square Knots.

13. Label the strings one to twelve once more, move from left to right. Carry string one and put it over strings 2 to 6 at a 45-degree angle—dual hitch two-six strings on string 1.

14. Using chord twelve, move cable eleven – seventeen at 45 degrees tilt on the 12th cord, double half hitch strings eleven-seven. And double half hitch string one through string Twelve to seal the tip of the knot.

15. You're prepared to make the lower part of the belt. Label the strings from one to twelve and move from left to right. Use the anchor strings 6 and 7. Consider taking thread six and take it at 45 ° all over string five to one. Twice hitch five-one cords on chord 6.

16. Consider taking string seven at a 45° angle and carry it through string eight-twelve. On string seven twice half hitch strings eight-twelve.

17. Take four major strings at the base of the "V" and make a square knot while using the exterior cords as knotting strings and the two center strings as filled strings.

18. Replicate step nine and step ten to the same set of knots you have produced before. Finish the sequence on a double-knot sequence. Introduce yet another Square Knot immediately below and in the middle of the last two knots as you meet the final set of 2 Knot Knots. You must make a "V" of Knots Square.

19. 2 times repeat step thirteen and step fourteen for a double hitch row.

20. Label straps one-twelve and move from left to right. Start taking strips one and two, eleven and twelve, split dual hitch, and thoroughly fuse out edges of straps.

21. Renumber the remaining one- eighteen cables, switch left and right. Connect a knotted square of one-four cable and five-eight wires, making you two knots square.

22. Strings three-six tie a square knot to the band of knots you developed in step 21. Continue this knotting process before the required guitar strap length is met.

23. Complete the project pattern by reducing the V. This is achieved by joining triangular double half hitch rows using step 13 and step 14. Once you start a new row, fuse one cord on each side and fuse the ends of the cording that has been lowered.

CHAPTER 9:

Patterns and Projects III

13   BUTTERFLY

Butterfly pin is straightforward and easy to construct and is a perfect thing for beginners. You could do more than one thing and share it on social media and relatives

Materials

- Hemp three feet of 1 millimeter
- Three beads made of wood, measurement V inches
- Tape
- Jewelry art pin
- Sticky bond

Instructions

1. Split the hemp rope to 3 lengths of 12-inch sections each.
2. Wrap the straps in the quarter and squeeze on your Macramé deck with a tucked edge to the bar counter or pin.
3. Move a bead on the string and move this from the fold about 2 inches.
4. Put the two other string branches and slip those underneath the crossed strands below the bead.
5. Create a square knot near to the bead by using a dual cord strand.
6. Move the knot to reach the initial knot. It forms the upper portion of the butterfly. Move the knot to follow the very first knot.

7. Place the following two beads on the string.

8. Drag the knot up to the very last bead and form the under feathers of the butterfly. 9Drag the knot into the last bead.

9. With the Last Square Knot, put a little sprinkle of glue. And let dry fully.

10. Split the two threads past the last knot.

11. Prune the anchor strings of the last knot around three by 8 of an inch. Remove cover

12. Just at the fold, remove the folding strings.

13. Tie a knot for each string to create the butterfly antennas.

14. Clean around the ties.

15. Stick the finished butterfly on the jewel pin.

14   MACRAMÉ NECKLACE

This one has that enchanting, beautiful feel! Aside from knots, it makes use of gemstones that could spruce up your look! Surely, it's one necklace you'd love to wear over and over again!

What you need

- Your choice of gemstones
- Beads
- Crocheted or waxed cotton
- Water
- Glue

Instructions

1. Get four equal lengths of cotton—this depends on how long you want the necklace to be.

2. Tie a base knot as you hold the four cotton lengths. Once you do this, you'd notice that you'd have eight pieces of cotton lengths with you. What you should do is separate them

into twos, and tie a knot in each of those pairs before you start knotting with the square knot.

3 Tie individual strands of the cotton to the length next to it. Make sure you see some depth before stringing any gemstones along and make sure to knot before and after adding the gemstones to keep them secure.

4 Take four of the strands in your hand and tie a knot on the top side of the bag. Tie strands until you reach the length and look you want.

5 Knot the ends to avoid spooling, and use water with glue to keep it more secure.

HOME ACCESSORIES

15   MODERN MACRAMÉ HANGING PLANTER

Plant hangers are really beautiful because they give your house or garden the feel of airy, natural space. This one is perfect for condominiums or small apartments—and those with minimalist, modern themes!

What you need:

- Plant
- Pot
- Scissors
- 50 ft. Paracord (Parachute Cord)
- to 20 mm wooden beads

Instructions:

First, fold in half 4 strands of the cord and then loop so you could form a knot.

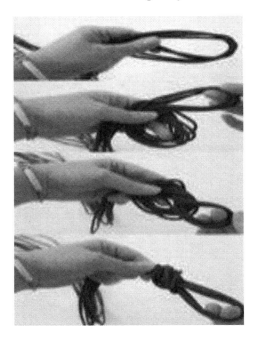

Now, divide the cords into groups of two and make sure to string 2 cords through one of the wooden beads you have on hand. String some more beads—at least 4 on each set of 2 grouped cords.

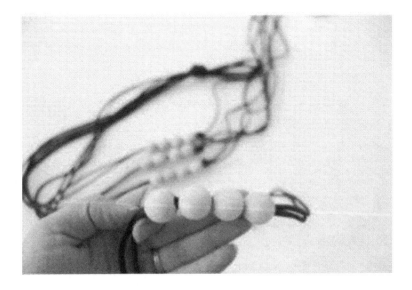

Then, measure every 27.5 inches and tie a knot at that point and repeat this process for every set of cords.

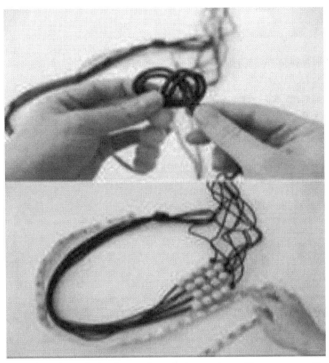

Look at the left set of the cord and tie it to the right string. Repeat on the four sets so that you could make at least 3" from the knot you have made.

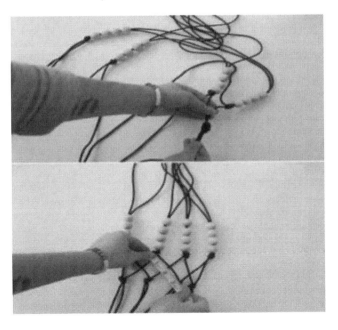

Tie another four knots from the knot that you have made. Make them at least 4.5" each.

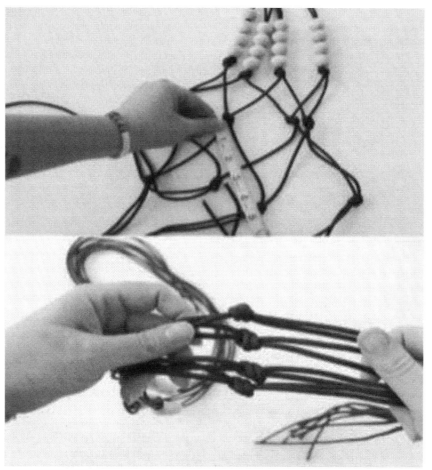

Group all of the cords and tie a knot to finish the planter. You'll get something like the one shown below—and you could just add your very own planter to it!

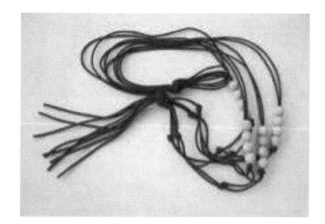

16   PLANT HANGER AYLA

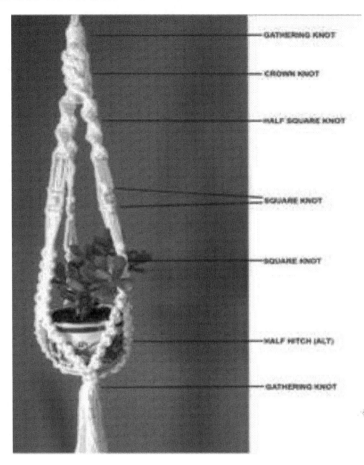

Description: Plant hanger of 2 feet and 3,5 inches (70 cm)

Used Knots: Square knot, half square knot, alternating square knot, crown knot, gathering knot, and half hitch knot

Supplies: 4 strands of a cord of 13 feet and 1,5 inches (4 meters), 4 strands of 16 feet and 4,8 inches (5 meters), 2 strands of 3 feet and 3,4 inches (1 meter), 1 wooden ring of 2 inches (50 mm) and 4 wooden beads: diameter 0,4 inches (10mm)

Directions (step-by-step):

1. Fold the 8 longer strands of cord in half through the wooden ring. Tie all (now 16) strands together with 1 shorter strand of 3 feet and 3,4 inches (1 m) with a gathering knot. Cut the cord ends off after tying the gathering knot.

2. Now follows the crown knot. It is the easiest when you turn your project up-side-down in between your legs, as shown in the photos. Divide the 16 strands into 4 sets of 4 strands each. Each set has 2 long strands and 2 shorter strands. Tie 5 crown knots in each set. Pull each strand tight and smooth.

3. Tie 15 half square knots on each set of four strands. In each set, the 2 shorter strands are in the middle and you are tying with the 2 outer, longer strands. Dropdown 2,4 inches (6 cm of no knots).

4. Tie 1 square knot with each set.

5. Then add the wooden bead to the 2 inner cords of each set and tie 1 square knot with each set again. Dropdown 2,4 inches (6 cm of no knots) and tie 6 square knots with each of the 4 sets.

6. Take 2 strands of 1 set and make 10 alternating half hitch knots. Repeat for the 2 left strands of that set. And then repeat for all sets.

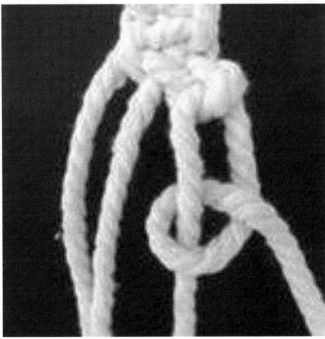

7. Followed by 3 square knots for each new set (so you have 4 square knots in total for each new-formed set).

8. Place your chosen container/bowl into the hanger to make sure it will fit, gather all strands together and then tie a gathering knot with the left-over shorter strand of 3 feet and 3,4 inches (1 m). Trim all strands to the length that you want. If you want you can unravel the ends of each strand.

17   PLANT HANGER BELLA

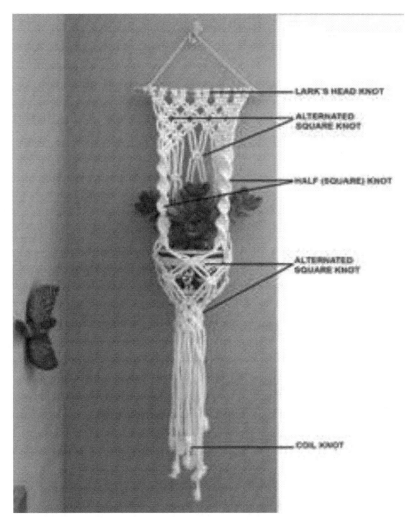

Description: Plant hanger of 60 cm (not counting the fringe)

Supplies: 6 strands of the cord of 13 feet and 1,5 inches (4 meters), 4 strands of 16 feet and 4,8 inches (5 meters) and a wooden stick of 11,8 inches (30cm)

Used Knots: A half knot, Lark´s Head knot, (Alternating) square knot and Coil knot

Directions (step-by-step):

1. Fold all strands in half and tie them to the wooden stick with Lark´s Head knot. The longest strands are on the outer side (2 strands at the left side and 2 at the right).

2. Make 4 rows of alternating square knots.

3. In the 5th row, you only make 2 alternating square knots on the right and 2 on the left.

4. In the 6th row, you only tie 1 alternating square on each side.

5. Then, with the 4 strands on the side, you tie 25 half (square) knots. Do this for both sides, the left and right sides.

96

6. Take 4 strands from the middle of the plant hanger, first drop down 2,4 inches (6 cm of no knots) and then tie a square knot with the 4 center strands. Now with the 4 strands next to the middle, drop down 3,15 inches (8 cm of no knots), and tie a square knot. Do this for both sides (left and right).

7. Dropdown 2,4 inches (6 cm of no knots) and tie 2 (alternated) square knots by taking 2 strands from both sides (right and left group). Then 3 alternating square knots with the other groups. These knots must be about at the same height where the strands with the half knots have ended.

8. Take the 2 outer strands of the left group, which you made 25 half knots, and take the 2 outer strands of the group on the right. First dropping down 2,4 inches (6 cm of no knots), you tie a square knot with these 4 strands.

9. Do the same with the rest of the strands leftover, make groups of 4 strands and tie alternated square knots on the same height as the one you made in step 8. Dropdown 2,4 inches (6 cm of no knots) and make another row of alternated square knots using all strands.

10. Dropdown 2,4 inches (6 cm of no knots) and make 5 rows of alternated square knots. Be careful: this time leave NO space in between the alternated square knots and you make them as tight as possible.

11. Dropdown as many inches/cm as you want to make the fringe and tie at all ends a coiled knot.

12. Then cut off all strands, directly under each coil knot.

18   PLANT HANGER CATHY

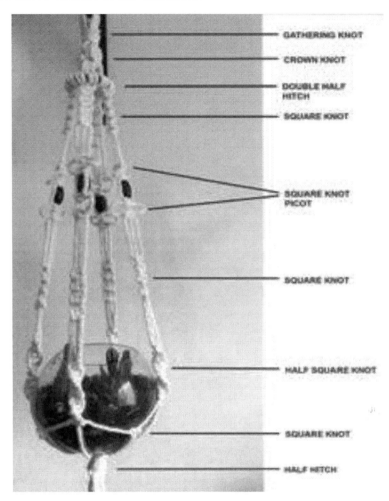

Description: Plant hanger of 2 feet and 9,5 inches (85 cm) - not counting the fringe

Supplies: 4 wooden beads of 1,2 inches (3cm), 3 inches (7,5cm) wooden ring, 4 cords of 18 feet (5,5 meter), 2 cords of 15 feet (4,5 meter) and 1 cord of 2 feet and 1,6 inches (65 centimeters)

Used Knots: Gathering knot, crown knot, (double) half hitch, (Half) square knot and Square knot

Directions (step-by-step):

1. Fold the 6 longer cords in half, placing the loops neatly side by side. Use a gathering knot for tying the cords together with the shortest cord. This gives you twelve cords in total.

2. Arrange the cords in four groups of three cords each. Make sure that each group consists out of 2 longer cords and 1 shorter cord. Tie three Chinese Crown knots with the four groups of cords.

3. Slip the wooden ring over the top loop and drop it down 1,2 inches (3 cm) from the last Chinese Crown knot. With each of the twelve cords, tie one double half hitch on the ring to secure it. This gives you a ring of double half hitches.

4. Arrange the cords into four groups of three cords each. The middle cord of each group is the shorter one, this is called the filler cord. Repeat step five thru eight for each group.

5. Tie four square knots, each having one shorter, filler cord.

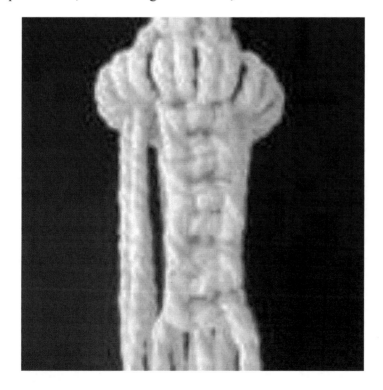

6. Skip down 2 inches (5 cm). Tie one square knot picot.

7. Slide a bead up the filler cord. Tie another square knot picot directly under the bead.

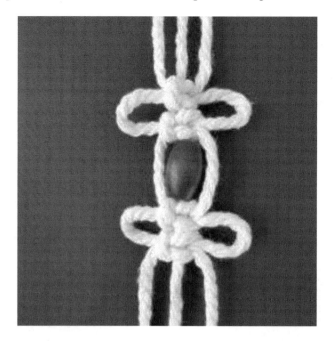

8. Skip down 2 inches (5 cm). Tie five square knots, each having one filler cord.

105

9. Skip down 2 inches (5 cm). Tie 10 half square knots, each having one filler cord.

10. Repeat the following procedure for each of the four groups you have just knotted: skip down 2,4 inches (6 cm); take one cord from each neighboring square knot to tie a square knot WITHOUT a filler cord. This gives you four square knots made of two cords each. The cords in the middle of each group are NOT used to knot.

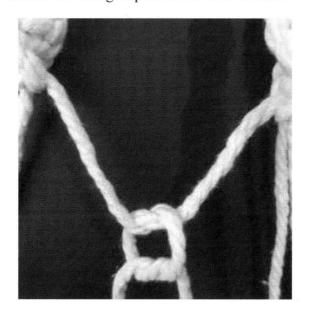

11. Skip down 4,8 inches (12 cm). Gather and tie all cords together with one of cords hanging using to tie 10 times a half hitch.

12. Cut the fringe to measure 6 inches (15 cm).

CHAPTER 10:

Patterns and Projects IV

19   SIMPLE MODERN DIY MACRAMÉ WALL HANGING

Here's one funny Macramé's thing. They may think the hanging patterns of the larger macramé wall are super complicated to complete, but trust me, they're not! It's an easy idea as long as you keep the knots and the overall design quite simple. That's exactly what this project is about macramé. The shape! It's extra-long and slim and works in those itty-bitty random wall areas where you need some texture. Or hang it out of a door. It's a decent size. It's a pretty little nod for your decor.

Materials Needed for Macramé wall hanging

- Macramé Rope– I have been using this 4 mm rope– 12– 16′ (as in feet) cords are required (twelve). Note that this is a thick hanging wall, which is why we need longer cords. To act as your hanger, you will also need 1 shorter piece of cording. Simply tie it on either end with a simple knot.

- A dowel or a stick– I used a long knitting needle. As long as it is straight and robust and as long as you need to work with what you have!

Here is the step-by-step guide for Macramé wall hanging

The first thing you want to do with each end is to knot a cord. For our project, this will serve as the hanger. Making a macramé wall hanging when its hanging is much easier than lying flat.

Begin by folding in half your 16′ cords. Make sure that the ends are the same. Place the cord loop under the dowel and thread through the loop the ends of the rope. Pull closely. That's the Head Knot of your first Reverse Lark. Repeat with the other 11 cords.

First, make 2 Square Knots rows. Now make 2 rows of Square Knots Alternating. Now make 2 more Square knots sets. Follow this pattern until you have 10 rows in total (2 rows of knots in a square, 2 rows of square knots in alternation). Working from left to right– make two half-hitch knots across your piece in a diagonal pattern. Now, from right to left– make double half-hitch knots across your piece in a diagonal pattern.

Have 4 rows in all. Make 2 more rows of knots of the square. We will finish the hanging wall with a set of spiral knots–

This is a half-square node sequence (or left-side square branch). (Do not end on the right side of the knot, just make square knots and spiral on the left side for you again and again.)

To build this spiral, I made a total of 13 half square knots. Finally– I trimmed in a straight line the bottom cords. The total size for the hanging of my wall is 6.5" wide by 34.

20 CURTAIN (FOR KITCHEN, SHOWER, ETC.+ VARIATIONS: EX: PENDANT)

Macramé Curtains give your house the feel of that beach house look. You don't even have to add any trinkets or shells—but you can, if you want to. Anyway, here's a great Macramé Curtain that you can make!

What you need:

- Laundry rope (or any kind of rope/cord you want)
- Curtain rod
- Scissors
- Pins
- Lighter
- tape

Instructions:

1. Tie four strands together and secure the top knots with pins so they could hold the structure down.

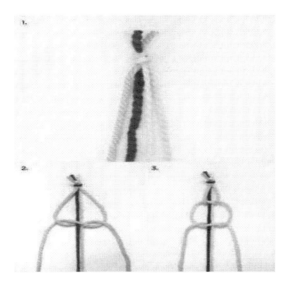

2. Take the strand on the outer right part and let it cross over to the left side employing passing it through the middle. Tightly pull the strings together and reverse.

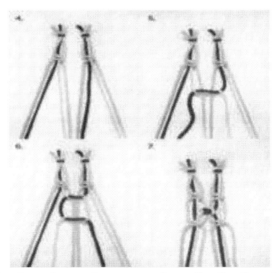

3. Repeat crossing the thread over four more times for the thread you now have in front of you. Take the strand on the outer left and let it pass through the middle, and then take the right and let it cross over the left side. Repeat as needed, then divide the group of strands to the left, and also to the right. Repeat until you reach the number of rows you want.

4. You can now apply this to the ropes. Gather the number of ropes you want—10 to 14 is okay, or whatever fits the rod, with good spacing. Start knotting at the top of the curtain

until you reach your desired length. You can burn or tape the ends to prevent them from unraveling.

5. Braid the ropes together to give them that dreamy, beachside effect, just like what you see below.

That's it, you can now use your new curtain!

21 MACRAMÉ SHOWER CURTAIN

What You Need

- 40 inches yarn of 40 sets
- Glue
- a pair of scissors
- curtain lace
- shower curtain
- macramé board

Instructions

1. To get started, use the glue to stick the lace to the shower curtain.

2. Make openings in the curtain lace where you see the nettings.
3. Arrange the cords on your board. Take two small cords and fold them into two. Attach the rope to the openings using the lark's head knotting method.
4. Attach other cords, to have a total of 40 sets.
5. Now, take the first two cords and entwine them to make a square knot.
6. Take the third and fourth set to make the same knotting method. Do the same with the fifth and sixth, and carry on with this pattern until you reach the end of the work.
7. For the second row, leave the first set and entwine the second and third like you have been doing. Do the same with the fourth and fifth, and carry on with this, until you reach the end where a set will be remaining just like the first.
8. For the third row, take the first set you left earlier and entwine them with the second, to make a square knot. Knot the third and fourth and continue until you reach the end, where there will be no cord left undone.
9. For the fourth row, leave the first set and knot the second and third, do the same with the fourth and fifth, and carry on until you reach the extreme where one cord will be left undone.
10. For the fifth and final row, knot the first and second set into a square knot. Entwine the third and fourth into the same pattern, and do the same with the rest of the sets until you are done with that row.
11. Now, trim the strands and behold the macramé shower curtain you just made.

22 TABLE RUNNER

Supplies:

- 12" wood dowel

- 16' 3 mm cotton cloth strands

- The hooks
- 2' of twine cotton dowel hanger
- scissors

Instructions

Step 1. At every end, keep your cotton twine and hang it from your door hooks. Fold half of the first 16" rope strand and build a dowel knot.

Step 2. Keep adding a 16" rope beam with a lark headnote to a total of 22. You should then operate with 44 strands.

Step 3. Pull the right outer rope through other ropes (left) and drape the end of the handle of the lock. It would form the basis for the next row of knots called a half hitch, creating a horizontal line. Use the second seam from the right hand to tie a single knot around the bottom, under the dowel around 6".

Step 4. To tie the base strand with a second knot, use the same strand. This is called a half-hitch knot.

Step 5. Make sure they are even and consistent.

Step 6. Repeat the second, third, and fourth ropes from the outside, tie up another half-hit knot to make it cool, etc. You'll start to see the pattern. This is a horizontal half-hitch.

Step 7. Keep wrapping consecutive cords in a knot. You don't want it to take the width at the edges nearly enough.

Step 8. Using the external four strands from the right again and make a square knot around 1.5" underneath the horizontal knots.

Step 9. Take the next four strands (five to eight) and make another square knot with 9 to 12 strands. Keep skipping four and tie four before you get done.

Step 10. Right again, use all four strands and tie the knot of around 3" under the dowel.

Step 11. Hold four square knots sets skipped until this row is done.

Step 12. Transfer to the right the two outer strands. Then use three to six strands in step 7 below the horizontal knot lines to create another 11″ knot. Use the next four strands to make a new knot of the square about 1.5.

Step 13. Start as shown. You won't do anything with the last two threads.

Step 14. Starting from the right again, create another line of horizontal halves, repeating steps 3 to 7

Step 15. Use the same rope base strand from left and create a hilly row of knots horizontally about 2.5″ below the last row. You will focus on it from left to right.

Step 16. Start from the left side, build a series of square knots with 1″ below the horizontal knots, without any strands. Then you build a second set of quadratic knots by skip the first two strands to the left. It is known as a knot that alternates. You do not want much space between these groups so that if you add each knot you can pull them together tightly.

Step 17. Continue to rotate until you have about 13 rows of square knots. This part is the heart of your table runner and everything else is what you have woven above.

Step 18. Add a horizontal half-hitch knots row from the outside to the right.

Step 19. Drop down about 2.5″ to create a new horizontal half hitch row with the same base rope from right to left.

Step 20. Turn right on this section two strands of rope, then tie a square knot of three to six strands. Skip strands seven to 10 and create another knot by using strands 11 to 14. Repeat so that you miss all four strands. You'll have six lines on the left.

Step 21. Skip the 1 and 2 lines on the left and attach 3 to 6 strands in a 1.5″ square knot below the last row. Then miss the next four strands and complete with the pattern the second-row square knots. It will leave you with six more strands on the right.

Step 22. Measure 11″ rights from the end of the horizontal knots and tie the outer four strands to the right of the knots. Keep the next four in a 1.5″ knot over the last knot.

Step 23. Repeat all over.

Step 24. Then tie the last horizontal knot half-hitch row to around 1.5″ below the square knots row, taking care as long as you like the ends on the opposite side. Remove the twine of the cotton from the dowel and gently slip all the lark knots. Cut the middle of the lark's knot and add the ends.

Your table runner's center is the perfect place for a center to lie down on the trivet and find some fresh flowers to anchor your hand. You can also use it as your own giant placemat in a breakfast bar to make your kitchen look amazing!

CHAPTER 11:

Patterns and Projects V

23   ROUND MAT (FOR TABLE)

What You Need

- Scissors
- macramé board
- cords of different lengths

Instructions:

You have to cut out five strings of sixty-five (65) inches, 7 strings of sixty-one (61) inches, and cut out other cords in the same manner of progression until you get eleven (11) sets of different lengths of cords.

Having gotten the cords, take out a single cord from the first set of cords and form it into a loop. Fold each of the remaining four cords from the first set, and entwine it with the loop. When you do this, hold the small remnant of the loop and the long side, and draw them so the loop will be lessened as much as possible. Arrange the knots and use a clamp or an adhesive tape to hold your work in place. Using the long cord, entwine the first cord nearby, to form a double half hitch knot. Do the same with the next (the other half of the folded cord) and carry on. Continue making the knots; as you finish working with the first four-folds, you will see a gap. This is when you fold one of the sixty-one inches cords into two and entwine it with the long cord. Continue with the double half hitch knotting. Form the knots this way until you get to an unusually wide gap. Fold another cord and entwine as you continue with this method. You should not only add cords when you get to wide gaps but also do the same when the cord you are using is not enough to do the double half hitch knotting. Continue with the knotting, as it goes circular in pattern and when you are at the finishing stages of the project, do make sure the tips of your cords are not seen. Hide the tips carefully. Do this check on both sides of your work.

This is to get a neat macramé table mat work. After you have done this, to bring the work to an end, take a measurement around the remaining cords to get a good circular shape. Cut out the remaining excesses and make fringes out of your remaining cords if you so, please. Your macramé table mat is ready!

24   HAMMOCK

What You Need

- Fabric glue

- Measuring tape

- Two 3-inch heavy-duty metal rings

- 6mm of cord material

Steps:

1. Let eight 4.5-yard cords pass through one of the rings and balance it by matching the ends. Let the cords be folded at the lower side of the ring. Another eight 3.5-yard cords should be put on the top and should be folded and balanced. A WK should be tied around the cords by placing in the right of the cords that were folded **beside** the ring, one end of a 50-inch cord. Fold the cord after moving it 2 inches down with the working end taken to the place close to the ring.

2. This working end should be wrapped around the cords, and also the end of the WC secured and wrapped firmly while moving forward till you're almost at the fold. This folded part should look like a loop, and the working end should be passed through it. The secured end of the knot at the top should be pulled which in turn will pull the working end and the loop in the WK. both ends of the cord flush should be trimmed with the top and bottom of the WK, and the stubs tucked where they are invisible.

3. Step 1 should be repeated, the other 3.5 and 4.5-yard cords should be mounted to the other ring the same way. Each cord should be carefully pulled so the ring can be tightly clutched without gliding on the ring.

4. The rings should be placed on the work surface or hung up. 2 very short cords from the right ring and the left should be selected and also lie close to the other coming out from the WK. These cords will be the holding cords for the upper region of the design. The cords should be diagonally placed to meet at a point.

5. The left cords should be numbered 1, 2 while the right 3, 4. They should be used to tie an SK with 1 and 4 as the WCs while 2, 3 are fillers. The cords for the back and seat will be mounted on both sides of the knot.

6. The ends of the 4 cords should be moved to the right and left lying beside the portion coming from the rings. Mount the cords of the back and seat on all 4 parts; this can best be mounted using a flat table for horizontal positioning.

7. A 7-yard cord should be folded in half and laid towards you on the 4 holding cords left of the SK. The halves should be put under the holding cords and towards you over the folded area, more like the reverse of an LHK. Some rooms should be left between the Knot and the SK on the holding cord. From the right half of the cord, a half hitch should be tied putting it right of the LHK. It should be passed over and under the holding cord pulling it towards your direction and tightened firmly. The other half of the WC should make a half hitch to the left of the LHK and tighten firmly.

8. The first WC should be placed by the right, so it lies against the SK. This process should be repeated for the other 7-yard cords making a total of 16 cords placed on both sides of the SK in the middle of the HC. Accuracy in measurement is highly important at this stage as well as the number of rows, so the spaces are correctly matched with the number of sides supports.

9. 21 rows of ASK should be tied as we make the back of this design. The first row must rest against the knots used in step 5, and the others should be an inch apart or ¾ inches depending on your size choice. Tie the left SK in row 1 with cords 1-32 and 33-64 with the right. This should be repeated for the odd-numbered rows. The left SK in row 2 should be tied with cords 3-34 and 35-62 with the right, repeating this for even-numbered rows.

10. The knots in row 22 should be well-tightened and lying half-inch below row 21 as we start the seats. This should be done for the other rows. For a tighter wave, the knots can be arranged ¼ inch apart, but the panel must stretch sideways, and the knots shouldn't be tied close to one another, so the panels don't become too narrow. The process should stop after tying 23 rows.

11. The rings should be used to hand the hammock chairs and two of the long side supports from the right and left each should be selected, and the four selected cords should be diagonally moved facing one another as was done in step 3. Down the WK, about 60 inches should be measured, and it is at this point the cords should come together. The SK should be tied to connect them for a while, it is expedient to put the seat on the HC to verify how deep the hammock chair is because the seats should come up for it to be on an angle to the back but it mustn't be too high else it won't be comfortable. The place where the HC is tied should be changed so the seat can go up or down.

12. After the lower HC is rightly placed, the SK should be well tied as the glue is applied.

13. The ends of the new HC should be moved so two of them go right and the other two to the left with DHH. The only difference between this step and step 5 is the type of knot used. Moving from the center to the outside, you should attach the cords on either side of the SK. A BK should be tied with the cords so the knots can lie under the seat of the design beside the lower edge. The seat can either be done by passing the ends via the loops behind the seat, then trimmed a little (the minimum length should be 2 inches though) and glued to hold them together. The seat can also be done by trimming the cords with a fringe left for them to dangle. BK should be tied at the tips to avoid unraveling.

14. The other cords should be organized in a set of twos for the right-side support. Moving from the top to the bottom, you should attach them to the right of the back and the seat. The SK in row 42 should be beside the first side support, which is 2 rows above the bottom BHH. One of the long sides supports (4.5 yards) should be slide through space beside the SK, and the same must be done with the second in a separate space beside the

same SK. The side support must be straight and with minimal tension. Both cords should be tied with OK and tightened firmly for it to touch the back of the seat. Another OK should be tied near the first, and it must rest beside the Hammock chair after tightening. Before moving on, the ends of the front of the seat should be pulled.

15. Step 11 should be repeated with the last long side supports, putting them after every third row along the right of the sat. This should be repeated with the short side supports while working in the upper area that the rows of the SK are far apart. The space should also be every three rows and ensure that the supports are put very close to the SK even while the spaces are very large. Placing the support cords into the position below the whole right side and holding them with knots is very helpful as it can help you adjust the placement accordingly

16. Steps 11 and 12 should be repeated while attaching the left side support. There should be adjustments made to the knots if needed for the hammock chair to hang steadily.

17. From where you began, pass the end of the side support via some other space most appropriately further into the left. They should be tied together with 2 OK just like step 11. Another side supports should also go through this step on both sides. The glue should be applied to the knots after finishing and allowed to dry.

CHAPTER 12:

Patterns and Projects VI

25. LANTERN

What You Need

- twenty-two (22) cords with a length of six feet per cord
- scissors
- bulb cage

Instructions

Entwine the cords to the top of the cage using the lark's head knotting method. Take four nearest cords and make a square knot with them. Take the next and do the same, until you are done with the first row. For the second, take two cords each from two different sides and make a square knot with them. Continue with this method, until you have the whole body of the cage covered with the square knots. The knots should not be so close; they should be spaced out while they are being worked on. Knot the last cords to the base of the cage and adjust your work. Take the pair of scissors and cut out the extra strands leaving none with the work. This is how to make a macramé pendant lantern.

26. LAMP WIRE

To make a macramé lamp wire, you need to measure the length of the cord you want to work on, to determine the length of cord you will use. Cut out your cord and fold it into two. Place it around the cord just before the lamp holder. Take the left side of the cord over to the right and take the right under the cord. Pull the two cords to come out through the loops. To make it easier for you, fold the left cord over your four fingers to have a big fold. Do the same with the other cord. Take the left one over and the right one, under, and pull each side. Do this again, and you will notice that the pattern will be twisting. Carry on with the pattern until you get to the end of the cable. For the last knot, make a double half hitch knot and cut off the remaining cords with your pair of scissors.

27 SUNSCREEN MACRAMÉ HOLDER

What You Need

- Cord.
- Forklift.
- sunscreen.
- Thin, empty flask.
- Bookmark.
- Clippers.
- Flash candle.

Instructions

1. Cut five-string bits, about 20″ long.
2. Fold in half and tie the center of one big sweater. Tape down the knot to stay in place.
3. Divide the string into five pairs and knot each couple down to around 1″. Take another 1″ down, take one line, and knot it from the pair next to it with a loop.
4. Continue to cover the length of the bottle for about four rows of knots. Slide your bottle in to test the fit and the appropriate number of knots. For ease of use, I put the bottle in the cap side downwards.
5. If the fit is right, tie the first knot to keep the bottle in place, with all the threads.
6. Place each string over a candle overheat to melt the ends and avoid fraying
7. Add a carabiner (or keyring) to the top knot to finish off, and connect to your pocket.

The travel size bottle last year was enough for us all summer, but you can replenish it as desired. You don't need to dig in your pocket now anytime you need a drop of sunscreen.

28. YARN GARLAND

What You Need

- yarns of different colors
- adhesive tape
- scissors

- macramé board

Instructions

To get started, cut out a long yarn, cut out six (6) yarns from each one of the colored yarn bundles, and arrange them according to their colors on your board. Do make sure the yarns you cut are of the same length. Place the long yarn horizontally on your board and entwine the yarns to the long one using the lark's head knotting method. From the rear at the left-hand side, leave the first yarn, take the second and third yarns and make a square knot with them. Do the same pattern of knotting with the fourth and fifth, repeat this until you get to the end of the yarn, to complete the first stage. For the second row, take the first yarn you left earlier and square knot it with the second. Repeat this pattern until you get the second row completed. For the third, leave the first yarn and entwine the second and third, do the same just like you did with the first row. Complete the third row and your work is ready to decorate your home. Now, cut out a few inches of the adhesive tape and stick the macramé yarn garland to the designated part of the wall for it.

29.   BUNTING

What You Need

- long rope
- six cords of about ten inches for each bunting
- scissors
- adhesive tape
- macramé board

Instructions

Depending on the number of buntings you want to make, cut out that number by six. Arrange your cords on your board and get to work. Entwine the eight cords to the long rope using the lark's head knotting method. Take the first four cords from the rear at the left-hand side and entwine them using the square knotting method. Make the same knot with the rest of the cords, to get a total of three-square knots on that row. For the second row, leave the first two cords from the left and entwine the nearest four using the same knotting pattern. Entwine the other two nearest cords too, leaving the last two cords undone.

For the third and last row, leave the first four cords from both sides and entwine the four in the middle like the others. Now, divide the cords into two parts, to have six cords on each side. Take the first two cords from the left, make a double half hitch knot with them, and go with diagonal double half hitch knots until you are done with that half. Do the same on the other side (right-hand side). From each half, take two cords in the middle and make a square knot with them. With your pair of scissors, carefully and neatly trim the strands so they will be shaped to have a pointed end. Using this same pattern, make other buntings and hang it. This is a detailed step-by-step method of making a simple macramé bunting.

30.   MINI MACRAMÉ SUCCULENT EGG DECORATIONS

What You Need

- ten (10) long cords
- ring
- tape measure
- scissors
- a vase containing the succulent plant itself

Instructions

Out of the ten cords, pass eight cords through the ring and make sure they are of equal sizes before you begin with the actual work. When the cords pass through the ring, you now have sixteen (16) cords. Take another cord and tie the cords with it carefully and neatly. This is to hold the cords in place, and also to give the work an aesthetic look. When this is done, divide the cords into four, to have four cords on each side. Take the four cords and make two right half square knots (spiral knots). The length of the spiral knots you just made should be about six (6) inches. Make other sets to get to this level and then, let the cords go free without any pattern on it for another length of six inches. Make an ocean plait knot here and let the cords go free again for another six inches.

This time, make the spiral knots to go through the left (two left half square knots) and then, measure the just concluded knots to make it be of six inches long. Do this same thing with the other cords so you will get them to this level. Take two cords from one knot, and another two cords from another knot, make a square knot with them and repeat the same with the other cords.

The distance from the spiral knots to the first square knot should be six inches. For the second row, take two cords from one knot, take another two cords from another knot and make a square knot with the cords. At the opposite side of it, take two cords from one knot, take another two cords from another knot and make a square knot. The distance between the first knot and the second should be four inches. At this point, carefully arrange the cords underneath the vase; take another cord (the tenth one), and tie the cords with it carefully and neatly. Measure out six inches from the cords and cut off the extra strands.

CHRISTMAS ORNAMENTS

31. BOHO CHRISTMAS TREE

Supplies

- A few branches or branches of the garden
- Wire of jewelry or other ornamental parts
- A brush
- Fishing line hanging

Instructions

1. Break the yarn in 7-8 inches sections. Take two threads, and fold half of them as a loop. Place a loop under a twig.

2. Take the looped end of the other beam and move the ends of the beam under the twig into the loop. Connect the thread under the twig at the ends of the rope.

3. Once enough knotted strands are inserted, separate the threads with a brush or comb. The "almost finished" tree is a little weak so you have to stabilize it with some starch.

4. Cut them into a triangle and adorn them with small baubles or beads when the boho trees are high. I just made a little flower star joystick.

5. It takes about 10 minutes for a whole bunch to produce. I think they would make perfect presents or on your Christmas tree, you could hang them.

32. TASSELS

Materials Needed:

- Small wood rings-if you have that lying around, you can also bend some wire into a circle.

- Macramé cord – I was looking for chunkier tassels, so I picked a 5 mm cord. Use a thinner cord if you want something smoother and tinier.

- Scissors

- Wire brush for fringe

Macramé tassel hanging from cabinet knob

A spiral knot is just like a square knot, but if that makes sense, you just work one side or a half square knot. You don't complete a whole knot in the square. Only repeat a sequence of these half square knots, and you'll start spiraling your cording.

The measures are broken down here. Cut two pieces of cords in length each 48.

Using Lark's Head Knots to fasten your cords to the wood frame.

You will have four cords in there. Make your spiral knots and go down until you've got a little cord left. That's what's forming our fringe.

Unravel the cords and brush them to form a fringe. Use your scissors to put the fringe on even.

Take a piece of twine from bakers and thread a loop around a ring of wood.

You're done! These tassels do not take long to make, so this year I've made a bunch to put on our tree. My finished tassels each measure about 6 inches.

Showing a series of macramé spiral knots with fringe, you can still buy colored cording if you want different colors. You can also interweave some beads for a nice effect in there. I tried to do this, but the wood beads ran out!

CHAPTER 13:

Patterns and Projects VII

33.   FRINGE PILLOW COVER

What You Need

- sixty-two cords (62)
- measuring tape
- macramé board
- scissors

Note: The size of the macramé you're about to make should fit your pillow, so you have to measure the pillow to determine the size of the project you are about to make.

Instructions

Take out sixty (60) cords and place them on your macramé board. Place these cords vertically and make sure they are of equal lengths and in good positioning. Take out another cord and place it vertically on top of the cords you have on your board. Entwine the horizontally placed ones with the vertical one to make double half hitch knots. Count out the first twelve (12) cords from the rear towards the left-hand side, and divide the cords into two, to get six (6) cords on each side. Make a double half hitch knot with the first cord from the left-hand side and then, go with diagonal double half hitch knots until you are done with the first half (6 cords).

Pick the sixth cord from the second half, make a double half hitch knot with it and also go with the diagonal double half hitch knots until you are done with the six (6) cords. Go back to the other half, and pick the cord from the rear at the left-hand side, make a double half hitch knot and make diagonal double half hitch knots as you did with the other row. Do this same procedure with the cord from the rear at the right-hand side. Go back to the left, and do the same so you will have three diagonal double half hitch knotted rows. Do the same on the other side (the right-hand side). Now, you have to entwine the two cords at the intersection using a square knotting method. Do remember to have the knots and the patterns you make with them to be of the same proportion so the quality of your work will not reduce. Now, you have to pick the nearest twelve (12) cords and repeat the pattern with them. Do this until you have made the pattern on the rest of your unpattern cords. Go back to the first pattern you made, take out the cord from the left part of the intersection, make a double half hitch knot there and start making diagonal double half hitch knots, keeping in mind to distance the knots as supposed.

Do the same with the next cord just before the intersection and do the third with the same procedure. You have again, three diagonal rows. Make three diagonal lines of the same knotting pattern with the rest of the other cords. At the intersection of every one of the patterns you just made, take a cord from each of the two sides, make a square knot with them, and continue with your diagonal double half hitch knotting. Carry on with the pattern of three diagonal rows and a square knot, until you get your desired size of the work. Now, get the cord that was remaining after you put the others into work, and place it horizontally on your board. Entwine every cord with the new one using a double half hitch knotting method.

At this point, you have to another set of cords, and repeat the whole process you carried out on the work, to get two works of the same shape, size, and design. Now, with the aid of a needle and thread of matching color as your pillow work, stitch the works with your pillow in-between the macramé works. This is when to give your project its finishing touches. With a pair of scissors, carefully cut out the excesses from the edges and make fringes from them. Check all the sides of the pillow to make sure you gave the work the best look it can ever have. Your home just got a new macramé fringe trim pillow!

34.   TIE BACKS

These directions are for a tie back measuring approximately 40 cm (16 in) long, but the length can be easily adjusted: require 1,25 m (50 in) of elastic cord for every 10 cm (4 in) of finished braid. You may leave the braid plain or adorn it with beads. Given that the elastic cord is very rigid and hard to thread through when inserting the beads, it is much simpler to use a tapestry needle to create a route for the finer needle.

You will need

• 5 m (5 1/2 yd) 3 mm teal elastic cord • Swarovski Elements: XILION beads 5328, 4 mm pacific opal and chrysolite opal, 54 each • Seed beads 11 (2.2 mm) blue marbled aqua and silver-lined crystal • Nylon beading thread • Size 10 beading needle • Tapestry needle • Two end caps with 3 x 9 mm internal dimension • Epoxy resin adhesive

1. Cut a 45 cm (18 in) length of Referring to Knotted Braids: Snake Knot, work the braid on your snake knot.

2. Tie a knot to a beading thread at the end of a nylon length (or equivalent color), and thread 10 beading needle. Bend the braid from the end about 5 cm (2 in), so you can see the pattern of the cord between the loops on one side. Place the needle of a tapestry between the two straight braid lengths you can see.

3. Move the needle of the tapestry through the braid to escape between the loops on the other side. Leave the needle in place for the tapestry; this is the direction the finer threaded needle takes through the braid.

4. Hold the nylon thread between two lateral loops above the needle. Pick an aqua seed bead, a pacific opal XILION, an aqua seed bead, a silver seed bead, a chrysolite opal XILION, a silver seed bead, an aqua seed bead, a pacific opal XILION, and an aqua seed bead.

6   Place the beads through the braid at an angle, then take the beading needle back alongside the tapestry needle. Remove all needles simultaneously.

7   Pull the thread taut over the braid to protect the beads. Between the next loops thread the tapestry needle again through the braid, to attach another line of beads. This time the XILIONS order is inverted, adding two opal chrysolite and one opal pacific.

8   Repeat to add bead lines, stopping from the end of the braid about 5 cm (2 in) apart. Sew firmly in ends of thread.

9   Cut the cord to the same length, leaving the tails approximately 2 cm (3⁄4 in) long. Mix a bit of epoxy resin adhesive and put a cocktail stick within one end cap. Place two of the cord ends in the end cap and force the remaining cord in place using a cocktail stick (or awl). At the other end, repeat to add an end cap, and leave to dry.

35.   HANGING SHELF

What You Need

- material for the shelf itself
- eighteen (18) big and strong cords
- a long pole that will be a bit longer than the wood for the shelf
- rope
- scissors

Instructions:

Entwine eight cords to one end of the pole. Entwine eight cords at the other end too. Take the first eight cords and make square knots with the cords. Make the same knotting with the other three sets and have the square knotting to be of the length of your choice, depending on the strength of the cords and the weight of the items you intend to keep on the shelf. When you have gotten the length of your choice, drill holes at the four edges of the wooden material. Take the patterns you made through the holes and use the remaining cords to tie the closest two sets together. Tie the other two sets. Tie the rope to the two ends of the pole and hang it. There goes a fantastic macramé hanging shelf!

36. DREAMCATCHER (TREE OF LIFE)

This fantastical Macramé design is best to make that somebody distinctive to your soul as a present.

What You Need

- Single 4 inches ring of brass
- 6 meters of all strings, thickness 2 millimeters
- Fifteen Pony Beads
- Feathers

Instructions

1. Bind one closure of the wire to the band of the brass.

2. Cycle the wire across the ring and firmly drag it after every circuit. To begin the following line of the network, precisely coil the string about the first string. Proceed to loop until the expansion is the required shape in the core.

3. You can append the beads elsewhere in the layout while attempting to make the hair clip. Shortly before inserting the bead, wrap the string and then move the string into the bead. The bead is then secured within the layout web.

4. Once the web is done, you can handle the ring with the string. Lock a ring edge with a dual knot. Roll the ring's size with the strap and then paste the ends to be secured.

5. Put a slice of wire, which is six to eight inches in length. Append the beads anywhere, make sure you integrate a dual knot since the last bead. Move a plumb via the beads until it becomes snug. Connect the strap to the circle with a twin knot.

6. Choose an upper six-inch string perched on top of the dream catcher to hold the final piece.

7.

37. FELTED IPOD COZY POUCH

This cute little bag is made by combining macramé with felting, a technique that is very popular with knitters. Felting is the process of making an oversized wool item with the intention of washing and drying the fibers on high heat settings to compress and tighten them, giving the material a completely different, textural look. This bag begins with beautiful variegated Italian wool, and the felting process blends the colors for a unique look.

38. COASTER

Hoping to add some DIY home stylistic theme to your living space? Have a go at making this adorable little macramé napkin!

Macramé napkins are an extraordinary beginner DIY project for anybody hoping to begin on their first barely any macramé projects. This project will fill you 2 needs

1. Help invigorate your imagination and
2. It is reasonable and can be utilized.

This is an incredible macramé project thought in case you're hoping to make something reasonably without any problem. It's superb for those hoping to begin with macramé or the individuals who simply need to make some macramé liners. As a heads up, in case you're anticipating causing this napkin, to know it can get somewhat dubious with regards to knotting and knotting in a round shape. You will discover when working inside a circular shape, and you will frequently be required to continually turn and move the project around the task while you are knotting. It can get somewhat befuddling on occasion, yet with some training, you ought to have the option to easily float through the creation of these liners in a matter of moments. For this task, you may be required to know 2 knots – the lark's head knot and twofold half knot tie. The estimated time for this project is 60 minutes.

What You Need

- 4mm Single Strand Cotton Cord
- Stitch Hook
- Lengths of Cord
- 3 x 170cm 1 x 50cm

CHAPTER 14:

Patterns and Projects VIII

39.   DECKCHAIR

What You Need

- complete wooden deck chair structure
- sixteen long cords
- scissors
- macramé board

Instructions

Arrange the cords for this work on your board and start entwining them to the top of the chair structure, using the lark's head knotting method. When you are done with this, get the four first cords from the left and entwine them to have a square knot. Get the other four and do the same, until you cover the first row of the work. For the second row, leave the first two cords and entwine the nearest four to have the same square knot. Knot the following four and continue with this, until you reach the other end where two cords will be left undone. For the third row, entwine the first four cords and continue with this pattern until you have covered the row. Carry on with this until you get to the last part of the work. Take the first two cords, make it go round the wooden bar, entwine the cords with the other two to have the usual square knot. Do the same with the rest of the cords. Use a pair of scissors to carefully and neatly cut off the extra strands, leaving five inches. This is how to make a macramé deck chair.

40.   WINDOW VALANCE

To make a macramé window valance, you need to know the measurement of your window, so that the work you are to make will not be too small or too big for your window. The size of the window should also determine the size of the cord you will use for the project. As for the requirements, you need thirty-four big cords, a wooden pole, a pair of scissors, and a macramé board. To get started, entwine every one of the cords to the wooden pole using the lark's head or cow hitch knotting method. Take the first four cords from the left-hand side and make a square knot with the cords.

Do this until you have patterned the first set of your work. The spaces you leave in-between your cords and knots should be even; this is to give your work an aesthetic look. To go over the second stage, leave the first two cords from the rear at the left-hand side and take the last two cords from the same knot; pick the nearest two cords from the second knot you made above, and make a square knot with the four cords. Pick the nearest four cords, make a square knot with them, pick the next and do the same, until you reach the last cords, leaving the last two cords undone. For the third stage, take the first two cords that were left undone and pick the closest two cords, make a square knot with them; continue with this pattern until you get to the last, where you leave no cord undone.

For the next stage, leave the first two cords and entwine the nearest four cords from the left-hand side, using a square knot. Take the next four cords and do the same, until you get to the last cords where two cords will be left undone just like the first two. For the next stage, take the first two cords you left undone at the previous stage and do the usual square knots with the cords until you reach the last part, leaving no cord undone. From the last knots, you made, leave some inches or any length of your choice, and cut the remaining cords in such a way that every one of them will be equal. You may choose to make decorative fringes from the cords. Your macramé window valance is ready to be hanged!

41. FEATHERS

Charms and feathers always look cool. They just add a lot of that enchanting feeling to your house and knowing that you could make Macramé décor with charms and feathers take your crafting game to new heights! Check out the instructions below and try it out for yourself!

What you need:

- Stick/dowel
- feathers and charms with holes (for you to insert the thread in)
- Embroidery/laundry rope (or any other rope or thread that you want)

Instructions:

- Cut as many pieces of rope as you want. Around 10 to 12 pieces are good, and then fold each in half. Make sure to create a loop at each end, like the ones you see below:

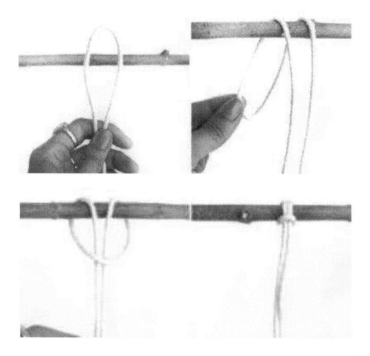

- Then, go and loop each piece of thread on the stick.

- Make use of the square knot and make sure you have four strands for each knot. Let the leftmost strand cross the two strands and then put it over the strands that you have in the middle. Tuck it under the middle two, as well.

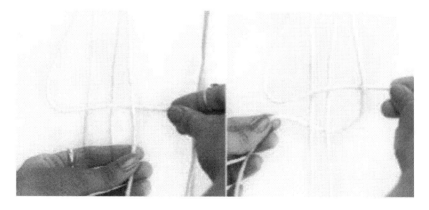

- Check under the strands and let the rightmost strand be tucked under the loop to the left-hand strand.

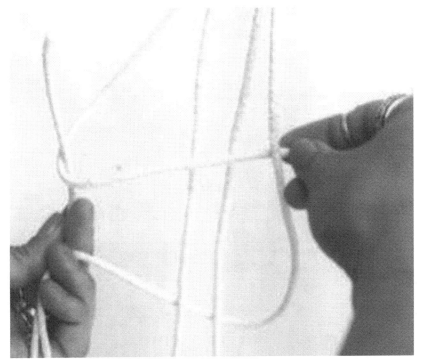

- Tighten the loop by pulling the outer strands together and start with the left to repeat the process on the four strands. You will then see that a square knot has formed after tightening the loops together.

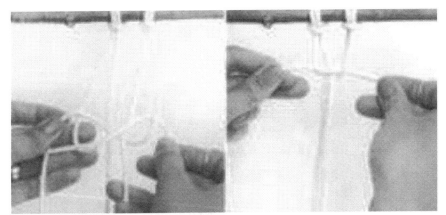

- Connect the strands by doing square knots with the remaining four pieces of rope and then repeat the process from the left side. Tighten the loop by pulling the outer strands together and start with the left to repeat the process on the four strands. You will then see that a square knot has formed after loops have been tightened together.

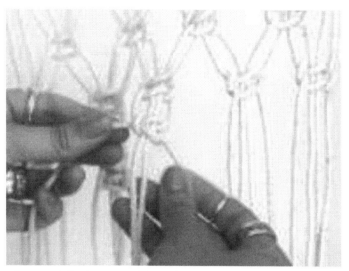

- You can then do an eight knot and then just attach charms and feathers to the end. Glue them in and burn the ends for better effect!

138

42. MASON JAR

Supplies

- Neon String
- clean Vessels
- Aluminum foil tray
- Washi tape
- Scissors
- Accurate knife
- Cold glue tool
- Tape measurement

Instructions

Step 1: Cut 5 strands of cord approximately 6' each. Fold them in the middle and tie the knot overhand, you should have 10 3' cord strands now. This is more than sufficient for a jar – change these lengths if your container is smaller / larger. Even the smaller jars with fewer strands and bigger jars with more strands can be compared.

Step 2: Use a cord or lighter to avoid additional spray if the cord is sprayed after it is cut.

Step 3: Tie two pieces together with your measuring tape from the original big knot. Repeat with the other branches.

Step 4: Repeat step 3, but split the joined strands and bind them together just about 2 "apart from the neighboring knots.

Step 5: Checking your Macramé net fit over the pot every time is a good idea. If you want to change how the net looks, you just untie your knots and make another test.

Step 6: Keep the knots tied to make sure your container is correct.

Step 7: Avoid the net approaching the mouth of the pot.

Step 8: Hot glue the two beaches in the jar on the lower part of the container. In the concentric zone, it is best done without touching the floor, so that the container would be flat.

Step9: Using the accurate knife to cut off the big initial knot.

Step 10: When the original big knot is cut off, the jar will be flat on top of the surface. If the rope is very thick, use hot glue to cover those raw edges.

Step 11: At the bottom of the pot, tie the string to the strings of the bottle.

Step 12: Use the same knife to cut off any excess material.

Step 13: Heat any raw edges to avoid scrubbing as before.

Step 14: Measure the jar's mouth circumference and cut the aluminum strip 1/2 longer; the jar thread will at least cover its width.

Move 15: After your aluminum bumps have been removed, flatter them by rubbing back and forth the handle of your scissors.

Step 16: There's no problem if still be some texture when you are done because this adds value to the surface!

Step 17: Using hot glue to protect the aluminum strip mouth of the container.

43.   POM POM HANGING MACRAMÉ

Materials

- Cord Macramé
- Fabric
- Scissors
- Macramé 4-inch net
- Small pan
- The measure of tape (optional)
- Pompom (optional) maker

Instructions

Step 1. Cut 8 bits of a 7-foot long macramé chain.

Step 2. Thread through the macramé hoop all 8 bits, and line up the ends.

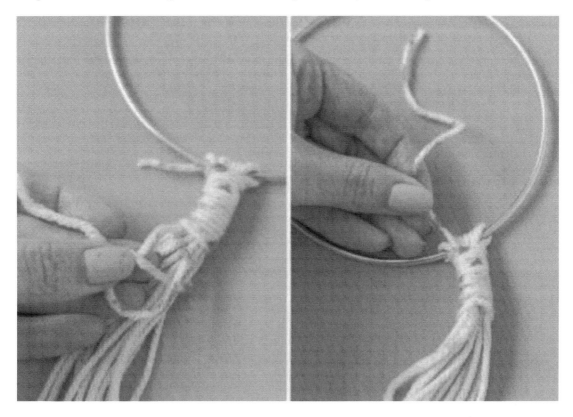

Step 3. Pull out some 24 inches of a piece of thread. Hold end at the tip of the hoop and circle the bottom upwards.

Step 4. Wrap the yarn firmly around both of the macramé bits and on top of the thread, leaving the string that you've just made clear. Cover before you reach the perfect length, then you are almost out of yarn.

Step 5. Thread the end into the circle and pull up on top of the strand. This will draw the loop upwards and protect the cover. Trim leftover thread.

Step 6. Separate threads into parts 4.

Step 7. Allow the first knot about 8 inches deep. Using a square knot. To ensure that every segment is even (recommended), you may either eye the marks or use a tape measure/ruler.

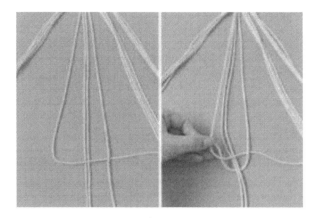

Step 8. I continue on the left (but that's perfect on either side). To make the square knot, cross the left side over the two middle sides, just under the top. Drag the right side under the middle strands and through the circle forward.

Step 9. Repeat to the (right) leg. That creates one knot in the square. Repeat on any group of strands five times, measuring as appropriate, so they're all equal.

Step 10. The fibers split. To build the next series of knots, take two from the right knot and two from left.

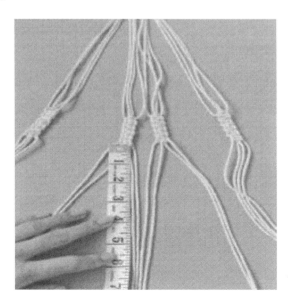

Step 11.   Measure another 5 inches down (give the larger pot more space) and make another 5 square knots. Repeat, removing individual group lines. Ultimately, you'll need to hand over the job to solve all the knots.

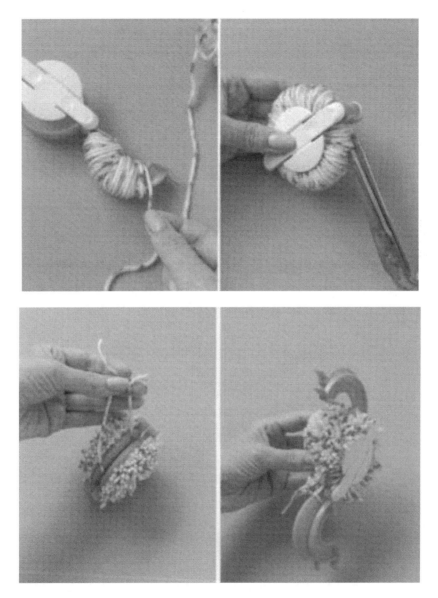

Step 12.   Now, make six pompoms!

Step 13. Add one pom-pom to the top of the hanger by knotting and winding it around. Add then four pom-poms to the first row of macramé knots by wrapping and knotting around the center ends.

Step 14. Place the pot in between the knots' second row, so that the knots rest around the pot. To keep the cup in place, repeat the tie knot from the top of the hanger.

Step 15. Then, tie a pompom to the bottom of the hanger and remove the excess string, so they're all even, around 6 inches in length. Unravel stops as you want to.

She's ready to sit now! Fill the pot and put the macramé planter back inside. Screw a hook securely into the wall, then loop the net around the planter.

Fill the pot inside the macramé planter and put it back. Screw a hook securely into the wall, then loop the net around the planter.

NANCY HARRIS

CHAPTER 15:

Patterns and Projects IX

44. DIY Camera Holder

Materials

- Cord macramé.
- Clasps swivel.
- The turns in clothing.
- Material barrier glue.
- Scarves

Make time: 1 hour (drying time plus glue)

Step 1: Cut the macramé cord in 2 lengths, 4 yards each.

Step 2: Fold through cord length so 1 yard is on one side, and 3 yards is on the other side. Attach the midpoints through the flat section of one swivel loop, leaving out the long ends of the threads.

Step 3: Push each cord's ends into their own circle and draw the taut around the knot.

Step 4: Continue tying a knot in the square. Take the leftmost cord (should be a long one), pass it over two wires in the middle, and under the most extended (other) cable in the right. So put the right cord under the two parts, and the left cord up & over. Push this squeeze—half of the knot in the line.

Step 5: Complete the knot in the square by doing a phase 4 reverse. Cross the right cord over the middle two and below the bottom, then cross the bottom rope under the middle two and over the center. Push taut and end a square knot.

Step 6: Continue to tie square knots until the best length for you is your camera cord.

Step 7: Cut the four cords to their ends. Insert all four cables into another knot that swivels. Place a dollop of glue at the end of each wire, fold the cords over the knot and keep clothespins in place until the glue dries up.

Replace the clips until the glue is dry, and pop the strap over your frame! For a camera strap, I love the macramé cord because it's super lightweight and sturdy, and it's relaxed around your back.

45.   "Owl" - A Beautiful Board With Its Own Hands Made Of Thread

This is the owl you get in the macramé technique after you finish the job.

At your discretion, you can use specific patterns to alter the appearance of the wise bird.

In any case, you must work:

- Cotton thread no. 10 - 10 meters
- Round sticks - 2 pcs.
- Colors
- Brush
- Eye beads two pcs.
- PVA adhesive
- Electrical tape

If the length of the thread is not enough for you (it will become tame during operation), tie one more. When they interweave, put a lump on the wrong side of the owl.

Cut the threads into ten segments - each meter. Attach them to a stick, so you get 20 threads as a result. To do this, take the first rope, fold it in half. Place the middle of this thread slightly above the rod, return both ends of the cable, skip into the resulting loop, straighten. Also, fasten the remaining nine ropes, resulting in about 20.

Glue the stick to the table with electrical tape to repair the work. To get the most realistic owl made in the technique of macramé, we start making it a front-end business. To do this, use the "checkerboard" form. Run it, so you get a triangular canvas.

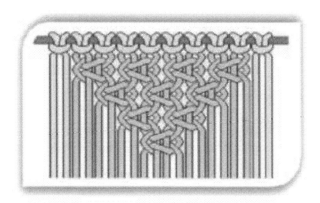

First row. Leave the first two threads free, weave 3, 4, 5, and 6 ropes and make a knot. The following threads lead to such a node as well.

Second row. Leave the first four threads loose and make the "square" nodes in the same way. You should also have four threads at the end of this row.

Third row. It starts with the seventh thread and consists of two square knots.

In the **fourth row,** make one highlighted element - in the middle.

Now you have to do everything in the same macramé technique. Beginner schemes are provided for beginners as well as experienced masters.

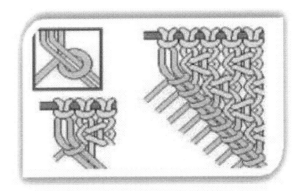

As you can see, starting from the right, from the first two threads, we tie a loop knot to the right. Then we do the following - from an adjacent pair of ropes and so on. Switch the upper part of the right eye of the owl. This element on the left also consists of 10 threads, but the loop node here should be on the left.

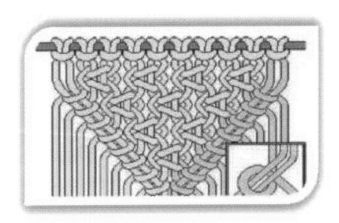

The description of the work on the macramé goes on, see how exciting it is to make an owl's nose with his own hands. For this, you need to separate the four center threads and weave four straight double knots from them - each consisting of one square knot on the right and one side.

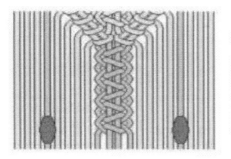

Count the fourth thread on the right and left. Grease their tips with glue. When dry, apply beads to each thread.

Tie a chain of straight knots into the hole one row more, then lower it so that the macramé weave helps the owl to hook its nose. These threads are also put into operation. And to complete the bird's eye, starting with the center thread, make looped knots on one diagonal and then on the other.

Then we do "chess," as shown in the diagram. It consists of the following lines.

- In the first a quadrilateral knot is twisted;
- In the second - 2;

- In the third - three;
- In 4 - four;
- In the fifth - 5.

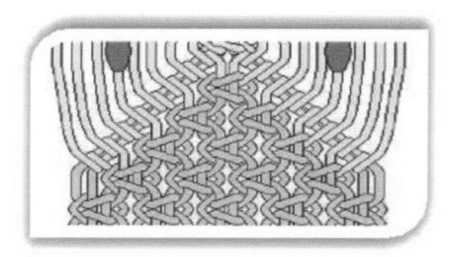

To make owl wings, follow the six double-sided knots on the first and last four threads. We weave "chess" from the rest, as shown in the diagram of the macramé.

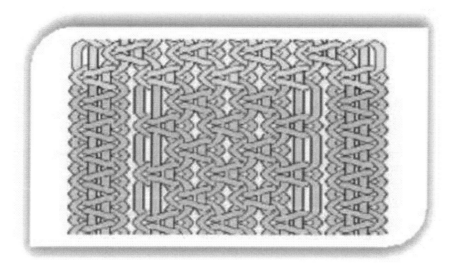

We tie the wings into "chess," weaving everything together with this pattern in two rows.

From 7-10 and 11-14 center threads weave one straight knot.

Put another wand under the deed, which will become an owl. Throw 3, 4, 5, 6, and 15-18 on this base.

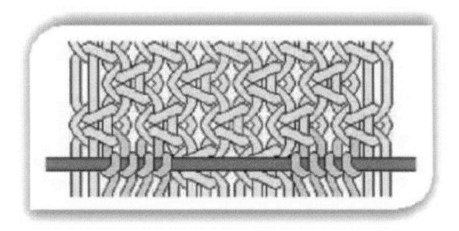

Next, weave to the end according to the scheme presented.

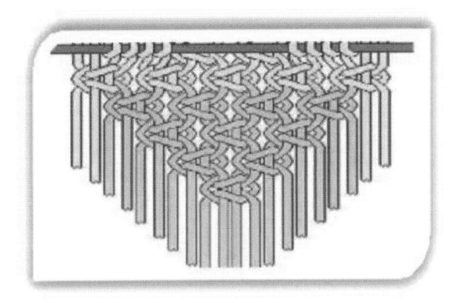

Complete five rows of "chess," you will eventually have one node. Cut the stitches diagonally from one side to the other and admire the stevia you have.

46.   MACRAMÉ FLOWER VASE HANGER

In case you're in any way similar to me and appreciate the fragrance of new flowers, you'll unquestionably appreciate making a macramé container hanger you can place your flowers in after.

Like the macramé key chain, this macramé flower container hanger doesn't expect you to utilize various knots. The knots utilized for this project will be your fundamental Square knot and Double Half Knot tie.

The main difficulty you may discover with this task will locate the fitting container size to macramé for this project. Other than that, a macramé jar hanger will be genuinely straight forward and simple to make.

This task is evaluated to take around 60 minutes. Contingent upon the size and state of your container, the time will vary.

When you have finished creating a macramé flower container hanger, you'll have a dazzling macramé piece you can put on a lounge area table, side table, or shelf.

Macramé Supplies Needed:

- Flower Vase
- 3mm Cotton Cord
- Line Lengths:
- 18 x 155"
- 2 x 18"

47. SCANDINAVIAN KNOTTED TRIVET

What You Need

- A ring
- two (2) long cords of equal length
- scissors
- macramé board
- four (4) wooden beads (will serve for aesthetic purposes)

Instructions

The length of the cord you need here depends on what item you need to make the trivet for; the same goes for the ring. To kick off with this project, you need to make a lark's head knot, which is also known as the cow hitch knot, to get the cords entwined with the ring. To make this knot, firstly, you need to hold your cords at one edge and place them underneath the ring. Pass the cords through the ring, encircle it, and pull the cords downwards before you tighten the knot you just made.

Make the knot in such a way that two cords at the right-hand side will be long enough to be tied when the project will be at its finishing stages. Take the two cords from the left-hand side, entwine them through the ring and pull the cords downwards as you did with the first. Continue with this method until you get the ring covered with the cow hitch knotting pattern. When you reach the two cords that were left earlier, use one of the cords you used to go round the ring and tie it neatly with one of the cords that were left. Tie the remaining two as you did with the first. To cut off the excesses, you need to make the lengths of the remaining cords vary. Take a wooden bead through one of the cords, tie it, and cut off the excess. Do the same with the other three, and have a macramé Scandinavian style knotted trivet right in front of you.

48. TOILET PAPER HOLDERS

What You Need

- eleven (11) cords of thirteen (13) inches
- scissors
- tape measure
- macramé board

Instructions

First of all, get nine cords, divide it into three, to have three cords on each side, braid the cords together. Get one cord from the two remaining, place it at one end of the braiding, make a loop with it, carefully and neatly tie it to that end, so it will have an aesthetic look. Do the same with the other cord at the other end, and you will have a new holder for your tissue paper. Not just a holder, but a macramé holder!

CHAPTER 16:

Patterns and Projects X

49.   INDOOR SWING

What You Need

- four (4) millimeter polyamide cord bundle
- lighter
- scissors
- macramé board
- a big hoop
- metal hanger

Instructions

Cut fourteen (14) cords of seven (7) meters. Use the lighter to melt the ends of the cords you will use for this work. Fold the cords into two and arrange them on your macramé board. Get the big hoop you will use for the hanging and tie it to a pole that will hold it firmly in place. Take a very long cord, melt its two ends and entwine it to the hoop using the lark's head knotting method for the first. Take another end of it and entwine beside it. Do this for the third time. Take the other ropes and entwine them to the hoop, just like you did with the cord. Bring two closest sets at the top together and make a square knot there. Do the same with the other three sets. This first four you just made will form the first row.

For the second row, bring two cords from the first row and make a square knot, get the second row and make a square knot with them. Do not shift any one of the sets close to the other. Maintain the distances so you will have nice work. Take the other two cords from this first row and get the nearest two cords from the first row, and make a square knot with them. Take the nearest two cords from two sets in the first row and make the same knot there. Do the same with the last one. The square knots should be tight. Take the remaining two cords from the last of the first row, get the nearest two cords close to it, and make a square knot there. For the third row, get the two cords from the first and second rows, get two cords from the third row and make a square knot. Get two cords from two different knots in the second row and entwine them to form the square knot. Continue with this pattern until you get the third row completed. The distances you leave in-between the cords and knots should be even. Like you did with the third row, do the same with the fourth.

Now, for the fifth, take the two cords nearest to the hoop and entwine them there to have the fifth row. Take the remaining two cords and the nearest two, to make a square knot. Carry on with this pattern until you reach the hoop on the other side. Entwine the nearest two cords there, just like you did with the other one. For the sixth row, take the two cords at the hoop on the fifth row, get the nearest two cords and entwine them to have the usual square knot. Carry on with the pattern until you reach the hoop on the other side; do the same thing there. For the seventh row, entwine the two extreme cords to the hoop. Continue with your knotting and repeat the same on the other side of the hoop. For the eighth row, take the nearest two cords to the hoop and entwine them there five times. Make the usual square knots. For the ninth, take the first two cords and entwine them to the hoop, continue with the knotting. Do the tenth row just like you did with the ninth.

Cut off the two cords you used to tie the hoop in the ninth row. Use the remaining two cords to hide them. Repeat the pattern until you have a complete patterned hoop. Now, it is time to make the sling. Cut out four pieces of five meters' cord and four pieces of ten meters cord. Knot the ends of the two sets separately, while leaving the hoops. Hang them together on the plant hanger and start braiding. Where the two meet, braid both sides for five inches on each side, and bring the two sides together. Braid the whole bunch at the same time using the square knotting method. Take one of the cords in the bunch, make a downward loop with it and tie it around the bunch tightly.

When you get to the loop, pull the cord through it and see that it comes out neatly. Take another separate cord, make a loop with it, and tie it over the tied pattern you just made. Now, divide the cords into four, take each set and make a long square knot with the cords. Do the same with the other three sets and make a very long pattern. Bring the patterned hoop you made and entwine every sling to the hoop. Neatly tie the strands around the hoop, and your macramé indoor swing is ready!

CHAPTER 17:

Patterns and Projects XI

50. HEART KEYCHAIN

Here to make the keychain you will need 8 smaller beads, one big bead, and 8 threads each 27 inches long.

Step 1: You will be making an overhand knot. Take one thread, fold it in half, now form a loop on top of the folded thread. This can be done by using your thumb as a guide to how long the loop should be. Then hold the thread at this length so that the loop is isolated.

Step 2: While keeping the loop isolated, create another loop with the rest of the thread and then place the original loop through the new loop while keeping hold of the original loop and then when through you can pull to tighten. You should end up with something like the picture below.

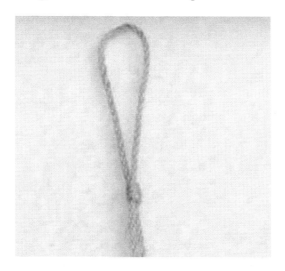

This is what your overhand knot should look like.

Step 3: Take another one of your threads, place it over your previous thread with the knot in it ensuring that the knot is in the middle of the new thread you have just chosen.

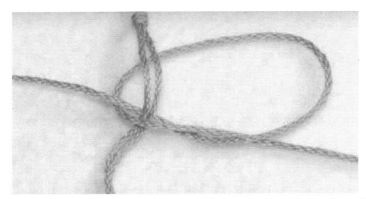

Step 4: Now you will tie a square knot. Take the left-hand side of the thread that you have just lay down (the one without the knot) and place it over the thread above it and under the thread on the right. Then take the right-side thread and thread it under the thread at the bottom and under the left-hand side and through the loop that has been created by the left-hand thread. Simultaneously, pull the threads on the left and right side so that it tightens, and a knot is created.

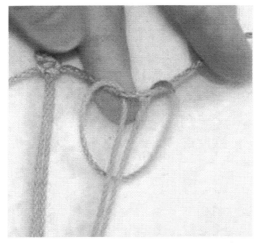

Step 5: Take the single thread on the right, place over the two threads in the middle, and under the left thread. Now take the left thread under the two threads in the middle and under the loop created on the right. Pull to tighten (both sides at the same time) and create your knot.

Step 6: Take the single thread on the left, then take the single thread on the right. Ensure that both threads are horizontal. For now, you will only be working with the right so you can set the left side down until later.

Step 7: Take a new single thread, fold it in half, make sure there is a loop created at the top. Then place the thread behind the single thread on the right and fold over the top. Now, pull the two loose threads through the middle of the loop so that it looks as above. Then pull the threads so that the thread tightens, and you will end up with a Lark's head knot.

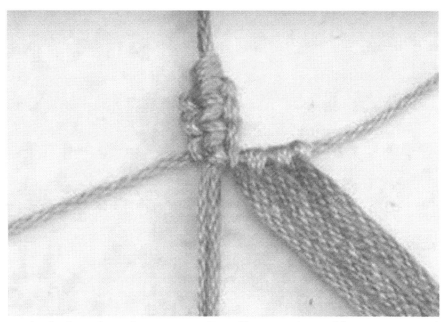

Take two more single threads and repeat step 7 until you end up with two more Lark's head knots on the right.

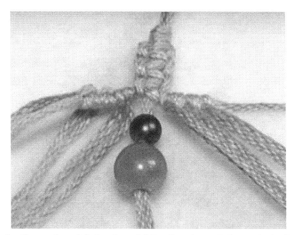

Step 8: Take the left single thread, which should be horizontal as stated earlier. Then create three more Lark's head knots on the left single thread. It should look like the picture above.

Step 9: Now you should have three Lark's head knots on each side.

Step 10: You should now have two threads in the middle. Take a small bead and thread it onto the two threads.

Step 11: Take a big bead and place on the same thread pushing it to the top so that your macramé piece looks like the one in the picture.

Step 12: Tie a simple overhand knot at the end of the middle thread, under the beads, so that the beads are locked in place.

Step 13: Take a pair of scissors and cut the loose thread at the end of the knot leaving just the knot.

Refer to the image above.

Step 14: From your left group of threads, take the first on the right and place it horizontally across the other threads in the bunch. Then take the thread next to it, loop it over the horizontal thread, under itself, then using the same thread loop it over the horizontal thread again and finally through the loop created. Pull to secure the knot tightly. You will have a half hitch knot.

Step 15: Repeat this step with each thread until you all threads on the left have been done.

Step 16: Take the next thread, directly under the half hitch knot, on the right. Pull this thread across horizontally and repeat the process of creating the half hitch knot.

Step 17: Repeat this process 6 more times so you have 8 half hitch knots in total like the picture below. (excluding the one at the bottom)

Step 18: Here you will be creating the knot at the bottom of the left side.

Step 19: Take the first thread on the right of the bottom knot. Then take the thread next to it, loop it over the horizontal thread, under itself, then using the same thread loop it over the horizontal thread again and finally through the loop created. Pull to secure the knot tightly. You will have a half hitch knot.

Step 20: Take the thread used to create the half hitch knot and place around both horizontal threads, under itself, then using the same threads loop them over the horizontal threads and finally through the loop created. Pull to tighten

Step 21: Then take the thread just used for the horizontal thread and place across the remaining threads. You should have three horizontal threads. Take the threads next to it and wrap it around the three horizontal threads to create a half hitch knot. Take the next thread and wrap it around

both horizontal threads, under itself, then using the same threads loop them over the horizontal threads and finally through the loop created. Pull to tighten

Step 22: Repeat this process, add one thread each time, until you get to the last thread. Your macramé piece should look like the image above.

This is what your finished left side should look like. If you have made any mistakes it is okay to go back and change them. The last half hitch knot can be hard to follow but use the pictures to aid you and you will succeed.

For the completion of the right side, start in the same way you did for the left side. This is the same process and if you completed the left side you shouldn't find it too hard. Repeat the steps given previously.

When completed it should look like the illustration given above. Don't worry if you don't get it the first time. You can always undo your stitching and try again.

Step 23: With the hanging threads from both the left and right sides, pull to make sure they are vertical. The threads should be together as one group.

Step 24: Cut a piece of the thread, around 4 inches, and fold it in half to use. Now place this piece of thread in the middle of the bunch but sitting on top and the two ends facing the top as in the picture (thread A).

Step 25: Take a single thread from the group of threads. Wrap it around the group of threads as shown above.

Step 26: Continue to wrap the thread around the group of threads until there is only a short portion of the single thread left. There should have been a loop created by the short piece of thread cut earlier (thread "A" in photo). Place the end of the thread (A) through the loop as shown, pull the two ends of the loose thread (A) at the top so that the loose thread (A) will come out completely. The end of the single thread becomes trapped inside the loop creating a knot.

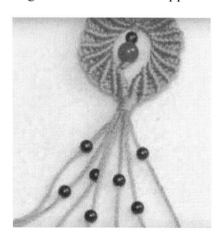

164

Step 27: You should have several threads hanging loose from the knot just created. Place a small bead through each thread and show them to have the same intervals between them. They should be staggered creating the pattern shown.

Step 28: Now do an overhand knot at the end of each bead to secure it in place. Refer to earlier instructions on how to complete this.

Step 29: Trim the remaining threads from underneath the knots.

CHAPTER 18:

Tips and Tricks

USING DECENT QUALITY ROPE

Let's start by saying that there are three different types of rope. You need to know their features to properly choose the type of rope to use for your project.

These are:

1) braided cord: this type of cord can be easily found in most craft stores.

It is suitable for beginners, in fact, it is made of strong fibers that give a strong grip to the project you are making. However, it is rather difficult to un-knot

2) 3-ply/ 3 strands: This cord is composed of three smaller strands twisted together to form a larger strand

3) single strand cotton cord: this is undoubtedly the best type of cord once you have achieved a good level of experience. The use of this type of cord will make it easier to cut it and also untie the knots.

There are two main things to keep in mind when choosing macramé rope.

- Cord composition: As we have already said, at the beginning of this book, there are cords made with natural fibers or synthetic fibers.

Examples of the first type are wool (from an animal source) and hemp (vegetable source). Synthetic fibers, instead, are made with petroleum-based chemicals. Nylon is an example of this second type of fiber.

- cord size: macramé cord can be divided into three dimensions:

small: it is a cord with a diameter of 1-2 mm that is usually used in the creation of small projects (e.g. bracelets) medium: this cord goes from 3 to 5 mm and is used for the majority of macramé projects, such as plant hangers and wall hangings.

large: this cord goes from 6 mm and up and is used in larger projects.

At the beginning, I suggest to use the braided cord, which is the most suitable for beginners.

Then, as soon as you have some experience, I suggest you change the cord and use 3mm single strand cotton cord. This way it will be easier to tie - untie the knots and cut the strings and fringe. In addition, your designs will also look better.

With a spool of macramé cord, you can realize up to 3 medium size projects.

KEEP IT SIMPLE

A good first knot to learn is the square knot. There are two ways to make this knot: The square knot and the alternating square knot. This knot is the basis of most macrame' items and is really easy for beginners to learn.

KEEP YOUR TENSION EVEN

This one has to be practice. The strength with which the knots are tightened affects the consistency of their size. Practice over and over until you find a rhythm and see your knots are consistent. You need to find a balance between knotting too loose and knotting too tight.

GET INVOLVED AND HAVE FUN

The easiest way to do something is to get proper help. The same holds for macramé-learning. Join a fellow member of the amateur macramé. You will find answers to your questions, will be inspired and will share information. Expressing your imagination by macramé is one of the best parts of the voyage. Let your imagination go wild, and construct something from the heart.

ATTEND A WORKSHOP

Teaching yourself is fun, but we suggest you attend a workshop if you have any in your area. You get to get in touch with so many like-minded people, and even leave with not only your very own finished work of art but also new friends!

SAVE YOUR LEFT-OVER CORD

You should make some attempts while you are training, and try again. And having the right length of JUST cord can be your biggest obstacle. You don't want a little string, because it can be hard to add extra to your piece. We also recommend that you make at least 10 percent more mistakes than you think you should, just to be safe.

SAVE YOUR MONEY

My advice is to always use a good quality rope to realize your projects. Obviously, a good quality string will have a higher price. However, you don't have to be afraid, I made for you a list containing (in my opinion) the best websites to order your materials from. In them you will find an excellent value for money and many offers!

- Mary Maker Studio (AU)
- UnfetteredCo (via Etsy)
- Rope Source (UK)
- GANXXET (US)
- Bobbiny (PL)
- Hobby Lobby (US)
- Uline (US)
- Pepperell (US)
- Ket Mercantile (via Etsy)
- Rock Monuntain Co.
- Niroma Studio (US)
- Modern Macramé
- Knot and Rope Supply (US)
- Knot Knitting
- Rope Galore (AU)

NANCY HARRIS

CHAPTER 19:

How To Start A Macramé Business

If you've thought about turning your love of Macramé into a full-time or part-time business, here are a few things to consider when starting a Macramé business.

DO YOUR RESEARCH:

We must, first of all, make sure that there is demand.

For this reason, it is important to participate in craft shows.

Also, it is good to take a look at craft marketplace websites like Etsy and Amazon. Find out if your items can be sold in one of the categories of these sites; if the answer is yes, then there is a demand. At the same time, make sure that there are not too many sellers selling products that are too similar to yours (low competition).

KNOW YOUR COMPETITION:

Before starting a Macramé business, it is essential to determine what the competition looks like. This means understanding how competitors have positioned themselves in the market and trying to differentiate from them. For this purpose, you could use different materials (e.g. sustainable fabrics), pay special attention to the quality of processing and more.

KNOW YOUR CUSTOMERS:

This will help you in the way you show your items, create perfect descriptions that are attractive to potential customers, understand which craft shows to attend and much more.

CREATE YOUR OWN WEBSITE:

It is recommended to create your own website. This is because it gives a professional touch to your business and is also a way to contact you. Then it is also a good idea to create your own website profiles on social media such as Facebook, Twitter and Instagram.

This will increase the visibility of your website.

TAKE GREAT PICTURES:

It is essential to take quality photos of your products. My advice is to allocate part of your budget to buy a good camera. Remember to choose a background with good lighting. Alternatively, you can also outsource the photography to a professional

ORGANIZE THE SHIPPING:

If you also sell your products online, you should also organize the shipping. It must be fast and it is essential to use good packaging material in order to avoid breakage.

It is important to take care of this stage because many of the customer reviews are about this aspect.

HOW TO PRICE YOUR ITEMS?

One of the most discussed aspects of selling homemade crafts is how to price your products. In fact, with a price too high no one will buy your items, while with a price too low you will not be able to sustain your business.

Here I will provide you with three strategies that you can use to price your items.

1) Strategy number 1: there is a formula that is commonly used for this purpose and allows at least a 50% profit margin.

   It is as follows: **materials + time + overhead costs** (e.g. warehouse space) = **minimum base price.**

   This price must then be **multiplied by 2.5 or 3**; and this is how you get the **retail price**.

   For example:

   retail material cost= $25

   time= 10h

   hourly rate= $15/h

   retail= (25$ + (10 x 15)) x 2,5 = $437,5

If you sell your products online, you should consider additional costs. These are represented by Etsy and PayPal fees. So, check on their websites how much these commissions are, and add them to the minimum basic price.

There are additional costs to consider even if you sell your products at craft shows.

These are State taxes and credit card fees.

2) Strategy number 2: **observe the prices of similar items.**

   Once you have an idea of the price range, set the price of your items right in the middle.

   However, if you use higher quality materials, you may set a higher price.

   If there is particularly strong competition, try setting a price a little lower than the middle price to attract more people. Then, once you have created a customer base, you can increase your prices.

3) Strategy number 3: first of all, measure the width of the weave in inches, then you must **multiply by a constant cost per inch**. A good range is between **10-15 $** per inch.

   For example:

   > retail= 25inches x $13/inch = $325

   Wholesale:

   If you already know that you will be using some materials in large quantities, you should consider buying your supplies wholesale. This will allow you to set a low price for your items and still make a profit.

NANCY HARRIS

Conclusion

One of the great advantages of this hobby is that with a limited investment in equipment and materials, you can get started with your craft.

The development of a macramé project can very well relax the face, mind, and spirit! Macramé projects require very little instrumentation and require supplies without chemicals and this is without question an earth-friendly craft.

Macramé is a great art and for good reasons has made a huge comeback: it's easy to learn, it's cheap, and it's simple to do. You will be knotting your way to beautiful bits in no time.

Throughout time, the potential of Macramé has been ignored. It was refurbished in the 1960s and the 1970s revitalized the old skills. It declined somewhat in the 80s and 90s, but at the beginning of the 21st century, its popularity returned to its full potential, with limitless artistic potential for hobbyists, artists, and appreciators of various diversified macramé products.

Today the hobby and skill of Macramé mean numerous things for different people. In several ways, the skill is gaining in popularity. And as an added benefit, your arms and hands can be strengthened by binding different knots.

Nowadays, a Macramé hobby means different things to different people. The skill is useful for many in a variety of ways. It can be very soothing to the mind, body, and spirit to build a Macramé project!

Made in the USA
Monee, IL
05 October 2020